8 Steps Forward

Latonya Henry

DEDICATION

I would like to dedicate this book to my mom, Debra Pierce, My dads, Anthony Pierce and Gary Wright, my daughters, Shaquavia Bowens and Rishiyah Mack, my God daughter, Kayla Woodruff, my sisters, Lakisha Henry and Olivia Pierce ,my grandson, Ka'worie Gambrell, my cousin, Michelle Copeland, my brother and best friend, Keith Allen and my sister-in-law, Tina Croft.

I would also like to give a special dedication to the leaders that have covered me through some hard times as well as good times. Pastor Rosze Kaur, Pastor Darian Blue, and my Pastor, leader, and spiritual father, Prophet Kuassi Lissanon.
A special thanks to my business mentor, Mr. Kevin Brinson. He has opened my eyes to what life is like whenever you focus on your mission and assignment. I am so grateful for the way that he came into my life and helped me redirect my thoughts to what needed to be my main priority.

Thank you all for praying for me through my struggles, for seeing the person that God created me to be, and looking past the person that I was in the world. Support means a lot to someone when you are trying to walk out of something that is not good for you, and walk into something that is best for you. I walked out of the world, and I'm so grateful to have had special people like all of you to hold me up whenever I felt like I was falling. People that did not remind me of where I had been, but reminded me to focus on where I am going. I love you all and you will never understand how much you really mean to me.

CONTENTS

INTRODUCTION

8 Steps Forward is a book that I wrote during a difficult time in my life. I don't think that I have ever experienced a time that I have had to wear a fake smile; hiding how I truly felt inside as much as I did while writing this book. Having to be quiet when I really wanted to spaz. Having to smile when I wanted to express how I felt.
This book shares the feelings and emotions that I went through while trying to figure out my purpose and identity. I knew the life that I lived so far was not easy. I also knew that God allowed me to go through some things to be a living testimony to others that may have been struggling with the same issues or test. But I just didn't understand my purpose. I wrote this book day by day while I struggled to figure out who I was created to be or what I was created for. I knew that I was Tonya from the hood (District 25) and I knew that I had some issues, but I wasn't sure about what my real purpose was. When the Lord told me to start typing, I realized that everything that needed to be written would come to me with the help of the Holy Spirit. I really didn't know what to say or where to start because I had been through so much to be so young. This book talks about my struggles, my strengths, my ups, my downs, ministry, relationships, spirits, regrets, and so much more. It also is very transparent about what I had to do to overcome life's obstacles and keep my focus on the mission given by God.
I am 37-years-old, and it is the end of the year 2016. I was born in Queens, NY and my mom moved to the south when I was seven-years-old so that we could have a chance at a better life. I went through a lot to get to where I am today, and I thank God for the grace that he has given me because without him, this book would not exist. I thought about throwing in the towel several times; even while writing this book, but God sent real people into my life to keep me on my toes and hold me accountable for doing what he called me to do for the kingdom. This book is basically my heart on the pages, pouring out to others to let them know that God is still in control and every plan that he has for you will happen no matter what the devil has in his plans.
My prayer for the reader of this book is that you feel my heart and understand that without God, we are nothing at all. But with God, all

things are possible. I am thankful for every obstacle that I made it through because they all made me strong enough to testify about them without feeling ashamed, and I give God all of the Glory and the honor for the person that he has ordained me to be. Today, I am an overcomer. I once was lost, but now I am found. God's grace has kept me through it all, and I will always glorify him for the gift of living.

THE ISSUE

Finding out what my issue was seemed to be a struggle for me. I had a hard time being accepted growing up, so I always thought that I was a problem no matter what the situation was. I grew up with feelings of rejection and abandonment, but I didn't quite understand the extent to what I was feeling. I never knew that the feelings that I had were wrong until I experienced acceptance. I had problems fitting in when we first moved down south from New York. I was picked on because of the way that I talked, and I wasn't very good at making friends. I can remember kids whispering about me on the bus because I even dressed different. When I was younger, children were very mean and they didn't know how to make new children feel welcome. I left New York, having to move into a different environment and not having any say so about it. Whatever my mother said was whatever I had to do. Besides, I was too young to make any decisions anyways. I was separated from my biological dad when we left New York, and I didn't see him again until I was around 19-years-old. As I look back over my life, I don't blame my dad or mom for any of my feelings that I've had through the years, but I do know that the separation from state to state played a big part of my feelings of rejection.

Rejection is the dismissing or refusing of a proposal, idea, etc.

Rejection communicates the sense to somebody that they're not loved or not wanted, or not in some way valued. I felt like I wasn't wanted and I never knew why things had to be the way that they were. My mom never knew that I didn't want to be in a different state and up until today, I still sometimes find myself asking God, "Why can't I move," or "Why did I have to move here?" After a while, my feelings of rejection and abandonment turned into anger.

Anger is a natural and mostly automatic response to pain of one form to another(physical and emotional).

Anger usually shows up when people don't feel well, feel rejected, feel threatened, or feel some type of loss. It doesn't really matter what type of pain or where it came from. The important thing is that the pain is unpleasant and it makes you feel uncomfortable. Any time that I felt uncomfortable, I had to do something about it. Whether it was best for me or not; I just had to do something to change how I felt. While studying about myself, I realized that anger is often characterized as a "second hand emotion."

A second-hand emotion is when you feel a certain way because of how someone else feels.

For example: When your friend goes through a heartbreak and it upsets you because it upsets them. I experienced a lot of second hand emotions because of my kids. They were dealing with a lot of feelings because they didn't understand why things were the way that they were in life. There were times that they would ask me "Mama, why do people do what they do, or treat people the way that they treat them?" My kids have struggled from heartbreaks and feelings of rejection or abandonment, and the fact that I had no control over other people's actions led me to deal with anger; second hand emotions. These emotions are emotions that don't happen directly to you, but they still affect you because they hurt someone close to you or someone that you love.

Anger is also known as a "substitute emotion." This means that sometimes people make themselves angry so that they don't have to deal with the pain. This was the issue that I had found myself dealing with for about 25 years. I had changed my pain to anger because it felt better to be angry than to be in pain. At first, changing pain to anger was done consciously, but I had done it for so long that after a while, I found myself doing it unconsciously. Being angry had become a lifestyle for me. I can remember people always asking me "Why are you frowning or looking so mean all of the time?" The truth was, they didn't know the issues that I was dealing with or the feelings that I had bottled up inside for so many years. They had no clue at all what my everyday struggles were. All that people knew was the way that they had seen me react to certain situations in the past. They knew about my attitude, my character, my demeanor and my temper. I was a person who was looking for love and needed empty places to be filled, but I wasn't quite sure in what area I was missing love. I didn't grow up with my biological dad, but my step dad was there to assist me with everything that I needed. I know that God chooses who our parents are, so I was over the fact that I had an absent parent. I had come to the conclusion that God does not make mistakes and no matter what, I was born with two great parents that God picked for me, so even though things did not seem fair to me, they were really out of my control and really not even my business. I had no right to question God about the plans that he made for my life or the choices that he made concerning my parents. He is God, and he is in control. He knows what is best for me; not myself.

After realizing how blessed I was to still be fortunate enough to have a step dad, I still found myself being angry. I couldn't figure out what the issue was because most of the things that I was missing, God had found a way to fill the gaps with something else for the time being. I had a loving family that was always getting together to show love and often, I was the person that planned the fellowship in love. My anger had become a permanent emotion. I was confused. I woke up angry and went to bed angry. There were a lot of times that I was angry because I couldn't figure out the reason why I was angry. Yes, I know that sounds real crazy but it's the truth, and I told you at the beginning of this book that I was going to be transparent.

Transparency is the key to getting the help that you need for your issue. There are many folks that will read this book that are struggling with the same issues and are not able to admit it, but the best thing that you can do for yourself is to admit that there is a problem and get help for it. I had to be real with myself. Dealing with emotions of anger were horrible and miserable. It didn't make things better when people would add fuel to the fire or do something to trigger the emotion. I was already feeling like I was not accepted and most of the time, being alone left me with feelings of abandonment. I felt so lost sometimes. I was so quick to give up on jobs, opportunities, friendships, relationships, memberships, leaderships, etc. because the truth was that I would much rather be alone and not deal with people any way. When you don't know who you are in Christ, or why you are going through something, it will leave you feeling miserable. There was a saying that my grandmother Ruby Ladson Copeland used to say and it was "Misery loves company." I guess I was different because my misery turned into isolation. I didn't want to be bothered, and I sure didn't want any company. After dealing with my issue of anger for so long, I thought that I had finally had control over it. I stopped getting angry and lashing out, or reacting in angry ways. Instead, I just started disappearing. I learned to stay away from people that I just knew were going to do, say, or try to find a way to upset me. I was easily provoked, and I didn't need to continue being triggered into my emotions because bad things would take place.

I figured, I was a grown woman, and there were some things that I had no control over, but there were also some things that I do have control over, and that is "Who I wanted to be in the company of." My anger had turned into isolation. I would go into isolation and sometimes people wouldn't hear from me or see me for months. I received phone calls from some family members, church members, or friends wondering what was wrong or was I ok, but I couldn't explain the fact that my lifestyle had changed from being angry to being secluded or confined. I started locking myself up when I didn't even do anything wrong. I started punishing myself and depriving myself of things that I needed to survive because I didn't want to be bothered. I had given up on life. I was so tired of people being used to me reacting the way that I used to, and I wanted a new start with a new impression that I had changed and I had self-control over my emotions. I tried to prove so much to others, but I had forgotten about God. God knew the real me. He knew that there was a person greater in me than who was in the world. He knew that I just needed to remain under the right teaching and get around people who had discernment. Having the gift of discernment is being able to differentiate between spirits. I had to get around some real people that were Holy Ghost filled and they were not focusing on what I had going on, but they were more focused on what God was doing with me. They were more focused on the mission and assignment as well as my purpose. My issue had no power over the power of God. My condition could not stop the calling that God had placed on my life. Being secluded just fed another emotion to take the place of the last emotion that I was trying to stay away from. Isolation had become a comfortable place for me, and I had found myself stuck for long periods of time; missing what God had for me because of my timing. I wasted a lot of time being isolated and going through unnecessary warfare all because of my conditions. When I met my spiritual leader Prophet Kuassi, he taught me some things that really helped me realize my true identity. He challenged me in a lot of things, and he held me accountable when it came to my life and wanting to be successful. I learned that success is not having nice clothes, shoes, cars, houses, degrees, jobs, money, etc. Success is being exactly who God created you to be. To be successful is to walk in your purpose. My pastor was more concerned about me being successful and living a fulfilling life in the kingdom. He cared more about my purpose and destiny than he cared about where I came from. He spoke to me about isolation the first day that I met him and he shared with me about every spirit that I was being attacked with. He told me to look up the lion and study how it attacks its prey. The bible speaks about the enemy in 1 Peter 5:8: "Be sober, be vigilant; because your adversary the devil, as a roaring lion, walketh about, seeking whom he may devour."

I learned that the lion sits back , watches its prey and waits until the prey is alone in isolation to attack. So as long as I was around other people, they were keeping me lifted up and encouraged. Positive people reminded me of who I was in God and how I was a conqueror. Being around others kept me lifted up and out of the state of depression. Whenever I closed myself into isolation, I became an easy target for the devil. I had to learn to keep moving so that it would be hard for him to hit me. My moments of isolation were so unhealthy. I can remember not eating for days because I had no appetite, and I would blame it on fasting and praying. There were some days that I was so burdened down that I couldn't even pray. I can remember crawling out of bed and the only thing that I could whisper was "Help." Tears flowing from my eyes and snot running out of my nose because I had laid there for so long helpless and wanting to just stay the way that I was because it felt so much better than having to deal with the world or life itself. It didn't take much for me to get fed up with people. I could see straight through folks and I didn't have a problem with letting them know once they had been exposed. I didn't like being artificial because it got you nowhere, so instead, I would just isolate and stay away; not knowing that the enemy was waiting for me to be alone. Isolation was not only a place to get attacked and a place to run away, but it was a place of abuse; self-abuse. I had a problem overcoming my issue, so when I finally saw myself getting better, I stopped listening to others talk about it or bring it back up. Instead, I started talking about it to myself. I started beating myself up about my issues. I became my worst enemy. I was dealing with condemnation. I had trained my mind to think that things were taking place all because of my past. In isolation, I found myself going in the past and convicting myself for things that I had already served time for in the world. God had already forgiven me for my mistakes, and he had forgotten about it. He was not going to keep bringing it up, so why should I or anyone else, for that matter? The bible also tells us how our sins are forgiven and forgotten in Isaiah 43: 25: "I, even I, am he that blotteth out thy transgressions for mine own sake, and will not remember thy sins."

Dealing with the issue was the first step that I had to take to move forward into the place that God wanted me to be in. We all have struggles. Some are worse than others. Some of us have habits, lifestyles, attitudes, secrets, and ways that no one understands, but the main thing is to figure out what the issue is for you because you can fool others, but you can't fool God or yourself. Deep down inside you will live with the truth that you have issues that you really need help with and you can't move forward until you have received the help to overcome some obstacles in life. Anger is serious, and people usually experience it when they are frustrated, unhappy, or when their feelings are hurt. They also experience anger when plans don't go as desired, or when coming against opposition or criticism. Getting angry causes you to act against your best interests. It never helps a situation. It has been known to cause you to waste a lot of time and energy, and it hurts your health. Being angry can cause delays, stress, high blood pressure, heart attaches or strokes. That's why it's important to have a plan set up to help you calm down and think before becoming angry. Anger spoils relationships and causes you to miss opportunities. It is a negative reaction, and if you wish to progress on the path of self-improvement or spiritual growth, you should avoid it as much as possible. I had to study a few steps to help me overcome anger.

Learning to calm down the restlessness of the mind and gaining peace of mind is one of the best and most effective methods to overcome anger and all negative emotions. Whenever you invest time and energy into things or habits that will help you get better, you will reap great rewards. Having peace of mind does not only help you overcome anger, but it helps you overcome anxiety and negative thinking. Peace of mind also enables you to stay calm in trying or difficult situations.

Peace of mind is a major part of not getting angry. It requires the development of an attitude of emotional and mental detachment. Mental and emotional detachment is very important for overcoming and avoiding anger. Detachment is basically an attitude of common sense and inner strength that leads to peace of mind.

Here are a few suggested tips that I studied to help me overcome my issues with anger. These tips had to be practiced daily with much prayer and faith that I could get better and have peace of mind to help diffuse anger.

1) I had to devote a few minutes to think about how my life would be without anger.

2) When I felt anger arising in me, I practiced breathing deeply and slowly to calm down. (meditation)

3) Counting from 1-10 helped delay my angry reaction and weaken it.

4) Drinking water when angry had a calming effect on my body.

5) I had to practice being patient, no matter how difficult it was.

6) Being more tolerant towards people, even people that I didn't agree with.

7) I made up in my mind that everyone is entitled to his or her opinion. I can disagree with people, but still maintain a good attitude.

8) I chose to react calmly and peacefully in every situation. I had to practice this over and over again, no matter how many times I felt myself losing control.

9) I had to practice self-discipline. Putting myself in time-out away from the situation until I could calm down.

10) Always thinking positive because it made it much easier to disregard remarks and behavior that could cause a reaction.

11) Don't take everything so serious because it's not worth it.

12) I had to learn to find more things to laugh about because life

is too short to not be happy and enjoy it. Practicing gratitude and being thankful for the things that are going well instead of focusing on all the things that are wrong.

CONNECTIONS

A detachment is the state of being objective; A separation.
My spirit was attached to some people and things of my past and it was causing a delay in my destiny because of my emotions. I didn't forgive for the hurt or misunderstandings, and I waited on apologies that I probably was never going to get. Some people left me, but they took a part of me with them because I never closed the chapters that needed to come to an end correctly. Studying these 12 steps helped me get better, and I was able to separate my feelings as well as be detached from the people and things that were holding me back in my life. I had to learn what soul ties were, and I had to pray for God to detach them.

I didn't realize that a lot of my problems with anger were because of who and what I was connected to. When I removed myself from different relationships, jobs, organizations, and friendships, I was able to see more clear and hear what God was instructing me to do. I found out that I was caught up with people that had me stagnant. They never encouraged me to grow. Be very careful of the people that tell you that "You are ok just how you are" or the people that tell you "Not right now" when it comes to bettering yourself. Also, be careful of depending on other people to get a word from the Lord on your behalf. You have to be able to hear the Lord for yourself and then you will have confirmation when someone else gives you a word. When God sends a word, he usually sends it in a way that you can confirm what he says because you will know that it is not just a coincidence. Just like in the bible there are certain things stated several times in different cases, but the word still remains the same. The word does not change or return void. I was connected to some people and places that really had me fooled and off balanced. I depended on a word from the people instead of a word from God. People that would speak the word, but not demonstrate it. I am very serious about my walk with God, and I will not speak something that

I am not going to follow. I'm not a liar or a hypocrite. I couldn't see the things that I was connected to because when you are connected, it makes you become it. A lot of times you don't know how much trouble you are in until you are out of it. I wondered why I would pray and fast and nothing really would take place. I was connected to some soul ties that were praying against me just as much as I was praying for myself. The only difference is they were praying curses. They were putting bad mouth on me and my life. Constantly speaking word curses or speaking negative. These people knew exactly what to speak because they were always around me or in my business. That's why you have to be very careful about people knowing your every move or knowing your weaknesses. I am not saying that the enemy has more power than Jesus, but the point I'm making is that the enemy does have power, and if you are not sanctified; meaning set apart, you will not be strong enough to defeat him when he sends his plots against you. God has the power to conquer it all, and we are made in his image, but it is the anointing that destroys the yolk. So, in order to break the connection, we have to work on ourselves. We have to spend that time with God and get the knowledge that we need concerning his word. That is what makes you powerful. What you know is what will help you when it comes to standing on your faith. The word of God will sustain you. I knew that there were some connections that were not ordained by God. Some connections that the enemy used to detour me and make me lose my faith in God. The tricks that caused me to get comfortable and share my dreams and visions so that others could either use my creativity or kill my dream and say that God gave it to them. Some things just have to be taken to God, and *only God*. You can't expect people to treat you the way that God will. God is a man of integrity. Most people are not! They talk about it, but their actions are not what they say. People have hidden agendas and they only share with you what they want you to know, and half of that is lies. I figured out the things that upset me about people that had caused me to stay away and most of it was people being unfair and unreal. They would do things according to how they felt or depending on who it was, instead of things being based on the word of God.

Being connected to different spirits will cause you to feel lost or delusional because one minute you feel good, and the next you are confused. These evil spirits come to drain the anointing.   These connections were with people that would say things like "I'm sorry but you know I don't wish you any harm," or "I want you to know I tried." Most people who try, succeed. So I hate to sound so cruel, but I'm going to be straight up when I say, if they have to tell me that they tried, then they didn't, and if you have to apologize, then you know you did something wrong. Now I have met some genuine people in my life, and I know for sure that they know my heart and they know God. When we are together, we don't always agree, but we understand each other as well as know the call on each other's lives. We have the Holy Spirit dwelling in us so we agree to disagree. Therefore, we understand the attacks on our lives and there is nothing that we will allow to harm each other or come between us. It is very important to pray about your connections because they will either wake up what is inside of you, or kill it. I'm tired of connecting with people that kill what God has planted inside of me. They can cause my visions to become blurry or they can cause me to abort what I am carrying from God. From here on out, I am very careful about my connections and I know that they play a major part in being delivered from my issues. Whatever you are struggling with can be revealed very easily by doing an evaluation on yourself and the things that you are connected to. It is possible to be around someone or something and not be connected. Doctors take care of sick people all of the time and they go home feeling just fine because they did what they were called to do without taking the problem home with them.

A connection is a relationship in which a person, thing, or idea is linked or associated with.

This definition makes me think about "Guilty by association." A connection is basically being linked together in a certain way. If you are not that thing that you hate so much, then why are you connected to it? Why do you spend so much time with it? Why do you make room for it?

99 percent of the issues that we have in life are not always based on where we have been, but it based on what we are connected to.

This first step in my book "THE ISSUE" basically shares with you what I had to do to help myself overcome my issue that I was struggling with. I dealt with some things that a lot of others in my family also struggled with, but it was up to me to recognize the issue and do something about it. Life was so hard having to ignore the fact that I needed help, but it became much easier once I addressed the issue. With prayer and supplication, Jesus answered my call, and he provided what I needed to be healed. There are a lot of times that people don't think that they are sick because the sickness is not physical or able to be seen. But the worse sickness is the sickness that is hidden inside where nobody knows that it is there. The sickness that you struggle with and it causes you to miss out on the things that God has created you for. (your purpose) The sickness that quietly eats you up on the inside because you know in your heart that there is a problem, but you are fighting with your inner self instead of letting God heal you. You are dealing with pride because you don't want to believe that you are sick because when people think of the word sick, they think of death. Let the truth be told, when you are spiritually sick, you are spiritually dying, so the only cure for it is Jesus.

You are dealing with a silent emotion, because you know that it is there, but you can't see it or hear it. You can only feel it and you are capable of hiding it so that it does not have to be addressed.

A silent emotion is dangerous just as much as one that is loud or crying out. No matter what it is, it still requires immediate attention because every day that goes by is a day that you could have added something great to the body of Christ to help expand God's kingdom. When you expand God's kingdom, he enlarges your territory. You just have to use your time here on earth wisely because tomorrow is not promised.

Time is precious and we all were born with a purpose. Our issues or struggles were already figured out at the cross and Jesus arose on the third day with solutions to every problem that we come up against. Trust Jesus to be the solution to your issues; I did. Because Jesus lives, I am no longer walking in fear or feeling the need to defend myself when the devil says otherwise. I know what the word says, and I know that it does not return void. So, because of that, I can walk in peace. I may come up against trials and tribulations, but I still can have joy through it all.

John 16:33: "These words I have spoken to you, so that in me you may have peace. In the world ye shall have tribulation: but be of good cheer; I have overcome the world."

Figuring out what my issue was, helped me to get to the next step in my life. I faced my demons head up and I sought the help that I needed to overcome anger and disconnect from connections that were not ordained by God.

SALVATION

Growing up, I was taught that Salvation is deliverance from sin and its consequences, believed by Christians to be brought about by faith in Christ.

Deliverance from harm, ruin or loss. Salvation is a source or means of being saved from sin.

As I have attended bible study and received better knowledge on the full meaning of salvation, I've gotten a different revelation on it.

Salvation is death taking place and being resurrected to have life. Salvation is not just about sin. As sinners, our sin was already forgiven when Jesus died on the cross. The bible talks about sin and how our flesh has to die in Hebrews 9:27-28: "And it is appointed unto men once to die, but after this the judgement:"

Hebrews 9:28: "So, Christ was sacrificed once to take away the sins of many; and he will appear a second time, not to bear sin, but to bring salvation to those who are waiting for him."

By reading and studying this scripture Hebrews 9:28, I understand it to explain that salvation is the resurrection. We have to die because of sin, and once we are born again, we receive the life of Jesus who lives inside of us from here on out. (The Holy spirit).

We as people no longer exist because we are sinners.

It wasn't the death on the cross that brought us salvation, but it was the resurrection that did it. The death on the cross symbolizes the sacrifice that Jesus made for us to even receive salvation. Because Jesus got up on the third day, now we have the right to eternal life.

Salvation is not needed to protect us from sin. It is needed so that Jesus can live inside of us. Christianity came because of Jesus dying, but getting back up from the grave, that is what gave us the right to be born. Jesus took care of sin when he died on the cross, so now we have to focus on him living in us and through us. We fall short, but that is where repentance comes in.

We have to live to show others that our worldly selves have died (just like the sacrifice on the cross) and our new person is actually a Holy spirit because it is now Jesus that lives in us, not ourselves. Once we make the sacrifice and die, then we will receive the salvation, which will be the resurrection of Jesus entering our bodies and living in us, so now we truly have life. Am I saying that we won't ever sin? No. The bible states that a righteous man falls seven times, but he gets back up. Getting back up symbolizes the resurrection that took place when Jesus stepped out of the grave.

I received salvation when I asked the Lord to come into my heart and save me. Once I did that, I decided to live with Christ living in me. I no longer had to say that "I was trying to follow Jesus" because I didn't have to follow Jesus if he was living inside of me. I am the light of Jesus and other people that are still lost in the world could be guided to Jesus by the light that is in me. If I have accepted Jesus in my heart and I believe that he died on the cross and arose on the third day, then I am saved. It was God's grace that saved me because I still fall short from time to time. I was asked "How do people do things of the world, and then say that they are saved?" I believe that just because someone makes a bad decision , that doesn't make them not saved any more. I did a study on this question and I came up with the conclusion that I am saved by God's grace and grace is basically the advantage that God gives us to override what the devil plans for our life. Grace is the free and unmerited favor of God.

Grace has given me favor in areas that others may not be able to walk in. I can tell when God has given me grace in areas of my life because things happen for me that are really not supposed to happen due to my rebellious ways towards Christ. No matter what I do, God still does not change what he promised me concerning my life. Romans 11:29: For the gifts and callings of God are without repentance.

My opinion about a moral person is that a moral person does not understand that none of us are good enough to go to Heaven. The concept of a moral person without Christ in them is a false belief according to the bible. A moral person is one whose conduct is good or virtuous. It also means that you try to do what is right or good. Morality is usually based on religious laws such as the 10 Commandments. A moral person strives to follow these commandments and they think that by following these commandments, they will please God. The commandments were set up as laws so that we will know what does not please God, and we will be held in conviction whenever we go against them. But the truth is, without faith, it is impossible to please God. We will be rewarded according to how we "diligently" seek him, not according to how well we obey the laws.

Hebrews 11:6: "But without faith it is impossible to please him; for he that cometh to God must believe that he is, and that he is a rewarder of them who diligently seek him."

Diligent means *constant in effort to accomplish something; attentive and persistent in doing anything.* Someone who is diligent works hard and carefully. To be diligent is to be tireless, persevering, and do things with great care.

Studying about sin after being saved; I learned that a Christian that accepts Jesus Christ and continues living worldly, or in fact, starts to sin worse, basically does not understand the concept of grace.

According to the bible, there is nothing that we can do to earn God's favor or approval. We can never be "good enough" to earn the right to go to Heaven. There is only one man who is righteous and has fulfilled the word of God and that is the Lord Jesus Christ. So, when we turn our lives over to Jesus, it is by God's grace that we have eternal life and can enter Heaven.

Ephesians 2:4: "But God who is rich in mercy, for his great love where with he loved us

5: "Even when we were dead in sins, hath quickened us together with Christ," (by grace ye are saved);

6: "and hath raised us up together, and made us sit together in heavenly places in Christ Jesus."

7: "That in the ages to come, he might shew the exceeding riches of his grace in his kindness toward us through Christ Jesus."

8: "For by grace are ye saved through faith; and that not of ourselves: it is the gift of God."

9: "Not of works, lest any man should boast."

10: "For we are his workmanship, created in Christ Jesus unto good works, which God hath before ordained that we should walk in them."

These scriptures are evidence that we are saved only by God's grace.

Sin after being saved is very much possible, but it is definitely not the will of God. Sin is never God's will under any circumstances at all. Jesus took care of sin at the cross. It's not that Jesus is not concerned about sin, but he does not worry about things that he has already defeated. That is the mindset that we should have today. For the record, God does not like sin, but he loves us. That is why he created us in his image. In Jesus's redemption is provision for every act of sin, condition of sin, as well as the sin nature itself. Jesus won 100 percent forgiveness and victory over anything that we may face in life.

Romans 3:23: "For all have sinned, and come short of the glory of God."

Christ's redemption has freed us from guilt. There are many benefits of redemption and they include eternal life(Revelation 5:9-10), forgiveness of sins (Ephesians 1:7), righteousness (Romans :5:17), freedom from the law's curse (Galatians 3:13), adoption into God's family(Galatians 4:5 , deliverance from sin's bondage (Titus 2:14 and 1 Peter 1:14-18), peace with God (Colossians 1:18-20), and the indwelling of the Holy Spirit (1 Corinthians 6:19-20).

I also studied more about redemption in Psalm 130:7-8, Luke 2:38, and Acts 20:28.

Ephesians 1:7: "In him, we have redemption through his blood, the forgiveness of our trespasses, according to the riches of his grace."

The word redeem means to "buy out." As I read up on the word redeem, I have learned that the term was used in reference to the purchase of a slave's freedom. This also relates to Christ's death on the cross. If we are redeemed, then our prior condition was one of slavery. Jesus has purchased our freedom, and we no longer have to live in bondage or slavery once we are saved.

Jesus paid the price for our release from sin and its consequences, so worrying about the attacks of the enemy is not a factor. He freed us when he died and rose on the third day. Once we are saved, slaves of sin now become saints, and don't have to any longer suffer as slaves to sin, or be condemned to eternal separation from God. Jesus paid the price to redeem us, resulting in our freedom from slavery to sin and our rescue from the eternal consequences of that sin. Just like I mentioned before.

When we receive salvation and we are born again, we die to the world and we become like Jesus. Our nature changes from the way that we were born, and it changes into the nature of Jesus. So therefore, we have the victory over all of the sins of the world, just like Jesus does. Our nature is how we live.

I've been stuck on the question "Do Christians sin?" The answer is yes. No matter how much we try not to, we still sin. Despite the new life within us, we still have to rebuke our flesh every day and try to stay on the right track. We have to be sure that our spirit man is fed more than our flesh. Our spirits are caged in fleshly bodies, and we are prone to sin. That's why we have to repent daily, ask for forgiveness, and turn away from it. Sin is tricky and many times we yield ourselves to it, consciously and unconsciously. We sin. Even though Jesus died for our sins, it still exists in the world. The closer that we get to Jesus, the more we will be convicted when sin comes to our minds, and we will think twice about it, but it is still possible.

The truth is God can't in a moment wipe sin away....Well, he can but, if he does that, then he would have to wipe away our wills. Then that would make it impossible for us to choose wrong. If God wiped away the possibility of sin, then he would have to wipe away righteousness, and we would not be able to use our wills to choose right from wrong. God would not know our hearts and our wills to follow him or Satan. If we lose the ability to choose right, then there will be no such thing as being wrong. I have discovered that Christians sin a lot and much more than some of us realize. The problem is that most Christians think that they have to be physically doing something evil to be calling it a sin. Some Christians think that sin is just an external act. Sin is a matter of internal attitude. Christians don't realize it, but the slightest lack of love in their hearts is sin and flawed in the eyes of God. Now, that is enough to condemn me, but the good thing about that is for a Christian, there is no condemnation, and sin does not condemn us. So, there is no condemnation for those who are in Christ Jesus.

Romans 8:1: "Therefore there is no condemnation for those who are in Christ Jesus."

This pretty much tells me that if I feel condemned, then it is not coming from God because he does not condemn us, ever. But that depends on if we are really in Christ or not. If we are not in Christ, then we are already condemned because we are already considered dead. We are dead until we are born in Christ.

Jesus speaks in John 3:18: "Whoever believes in him is not condemned, but whoever does not believe stands condemned already because he has not believed in the name of God's one and only son."
We have to believe in order to receive salvation and once we do that, we are safe from condemnation.

Learning more and more about salvation has taught me that the terms "save" and "salvation" were sometimes used by bible writers to convey the idea of a person being delivered from danger or destruction. We do not have to be afraid because the Lord will fight for us.

Exodus 14:13-14: "Moses answered the people "Do not be afraid, Stand firm and you will see the deliverance the Lord will bring you today. The Egyptians you see today, you will never see again.
14 "The Lord will fight for you; you need only to be still."

This refers to deliverance from sin. The son of God was created to help us and save us from sin. Once we have salvation, we are not thinking or making decisions on our own any more. The struggles that we had in the world may often come up, but we will not have to fight like we used to because the Holy Spirit is now fighting for us. The Holy spirit gives us the heads up about certain things that may be ahead of us or cause us unnecessary warfare. We just have to pay attention to the signs and warnings that he gives us because warning comes before destruction every time. This is why salvation is very important because we need the life of Christ in us. We cannot do it alone. We don't know what is best for ourselves and we have no clue what is planned in our future. The devil plots on a regular, but with the Holy spirit directing us, we have nothing to worry about. God is always ahead of the devil; after all, he created him too. We were born with a nature of sin so that is the reason why we have to be born again. Death must take place in order to be reborn.

Since death is caused by sin, people who receive salvation do not have to worry about death, but people who haven't received salvation will not receive the reward of eternal life. They will perish and burn in hell forever.

To gain salvation, I had to exercise my faith daily in Jesus and demonstrate it by obeying God's commands. Obeying his commands and having faith allowed me to tap into places that I never knew existed. From then on, I walked believing that I was healed of everything that the enemy used to detour me or destroy my spirit.
I had to activate my faith.

Acts 4:10: "Then know this; you and all the people of Israel: It is by the name of Jesus Christ of Nazareth, whom you crucified but whom God raised from the dead ,that this man stands before you healed."

I had to show acts of obedience to show that my faith was alive. I also served and showed God that my actions were the evidence of my faith. Faith without works is dead. I could not expect God to do everything for me when he had given me the tools to work it out through my faith.
James 2:24: "Ye see then how that by works a man is justified, and

not by faith only.

25 "Likewise also was not Rahab the harlot justified by works when she had received the messengers, and had sent them out another way?"

26 "For as the body without the spirit is dead, so faith without works is dead also."

However, this does not mean that I can earn salvation. It is God's gift to us based on his undeserved kindness or grace for our lives. God does not owe us anything; we owe him our lives. God gave his only son to sacrifice his life and arise on the third day so that we could receive salvation. Jesus thought enough of us to be obedient and sacrifice so that we would never have to experience eternal hell. I thought deeply concerning Jesus's sacrifice, and I tried to imagine myself in God's place. I don't think that I would've been able to sacrifice my kids, or better yet, my only grandson for the world to have everlasting life. That would be very hard for me right now. The closer I get to God, the more I see myself able to sacrifice different things in my life, but my kids…..now that's tough. I ask God every day to cover my kids and grandchild so that I won't have to experience the hurt that I've seen some others experience. I've been to several funerals and watched several mothers burry their kids. I have spoken at several candle light vigils, and I just don't think that I would be able to bare the pain.

Too many times I meet people who may have seen signs that God was trying to show them where the enemy was, but they didn't believe it, or they didn't have enough faith that God could turn the situation around.

There are times when God sends us warnings before destruction to give us a chance to get saved or make it right, but we fail to realize that our days are numbered, and we don't have much longer on this earth. I consider myself an alien to this world since I have received salvation. I don't belong here. I am just put here to work for God and once my work is done, I will be going home to be with the Lord. My focus is not to dwell on how much better I can be from my past experiences, but to be the best that I can be with Christ operating in me and directing me to my destiny. Having my faith built up allows me to move into the right directions without thinking twice about God's instructions. My faith helps me to keep my focus and believe as well as expect something to take place from Heaven. My focus is to spread the gospel of Jesus Christ and to be a witness of his word. My life here is numbered and I can't waste any time on things that are not going to help expand the kingdom. Many people don't focus on salvation or faith because it will mean that they have to stop doing a lot of things. Faith means work, and people don't like to work hard. They would rather keep living the way that they are and seek God when things get rough. We often take life for granted and we say "Well, let me take one last drink, take one more pull off of the drugs, tell one more lie, manipulate one more person, fornicate one last time, steal one more thing, gossip a little while longer, or hurt one more person by paying revenge."

Salvation is very important because until you get saved, you are in danger of perishing.

To perish is to suffer death, typically in a violent, sudden, or untimely way.

When I studied about what it was to perish, I realized that Jesus used the word "perish" or "destroy" all through the bible and the original Greek word for it is "apollumi."

This word means to "lose, or to be lost."

The word "apollumi" describes a sheep that was lost and was found and restored, and the bible stresses how a lost sheep is very important to God.

I was a lost sheep once because I didn't fully understand what the word salvation was. As I grew older in God, I studied more and more about what God consists of, and how salvation is set up to save us from sin or perishing, but also to impart a greater being in us.

Salvation is the number one thing that is important in my life. I have many things that I consider important like:

*family
*friends
*education
*a job/career
*a house
* health
*food
*clothing, etc.

21

But there is something that is more important than all of these. Salvation is much more important than having the finer things in life.

The bible verse Mark: 8:36-37 says: "For what shall it prophet a man, if he shall gain the whole world and lose his own soul? Or what shall a man give in exchange for his soul?"

This verse lets me know that I have something more valuable than all of the riches in the world, including the world itself. My soul is what has value. My soul is the real me.

My soul can be lost and losing my soul is like losing the whole world in God's eyes. The bible speaks about our souls being saved from Hell. Hell is where the gnashing of teeth and burning of flesh will take place. I don't want to experience the burning and gnashing of teeth. I can't stand for my teeth to even rub together the wrong way, and I definitely don't like to be hot!

Salvation is very much necessary. Everyone that is born into the world has to die one day.

It states this in Romans 5:12: "Wherefore, as by one man is entered into the world ,and death by sin; and so death passed upon all men, for that all have sinned."

When we are born as babies, we already have a nature to sin. It's evident by seeing kids at the ages of two or three as they start rebelling when parents tell them right from wrong and they do the opposite.

The book of Revelation speaks about sin and how if we are not saved from it, we will be thrown into the lake of fire.

Revelation 21:8: "But the fearful, and unbelieving, and the abominable, and murderers, and fornicators, and sorcerers, and idolaters, and all liars, shall have their part in the lake which burneth with fire and brimstone: which is the second death.

Revelation 2:11 says: "He who has an ear, let him hear what the spirit says to the churches. He who overcomes will not be hurt at all by the second death."

In this verse, Jesus basically promises us that believers, overcomers, or those who have received salvation, will not experience the lake of fire. The second death is mainly for the people that rejected Jesus. It is not a place that Christians have to fear.

The second death refers to the death after you die and leave this world.

The bible says that all liars will not get in Heaven. I totally get upset with people who lie or try to manipulate situations to make things work for themselves, but reading this verse lets me know that Jesus does not approve of it either. He takes lying very serious; along with sin, PERIOD!

The bible also states that if you steal something or fornicate, you cannot be a part of God's kingdom. We are the kingdom, and our job is to expand the kingdom while we are here on earth, but everyone will not be a part of it. This includes Heaven as well.

We all need salvation to be saved from these things of the world and I don't know of anyone that wants to burn in the lake of fire. Salvation is the only thing that excuses you from being thrown into the lake.

Hell is a place of God's wrath and no one wants to be a recipient of God's wrath. We all want to have everlasting life.

John 3:36: "He that believeth on the son hath everlasting life, he that believeth not the son shall not see life; but the wrath of God abideth on him."

Reading this verse made me think. The verse says that "He that believeth not the son shall not see life." That makes me think that the life that I live now is nothing compared to the real life that I will receive when I leave this world. This life that I live now is just to pursue my purpose that God has created me for and obey his commands so that he will see that my heart and soul is 100% in Christ. My purpose here is to allow Christ to live through me and use my body as a living vessel. The life that I live on earth will determine my reward in the end. The reward that we should be seeking is eternal life with the Lord. You cannot receive eternal life without getting saved. You have to receive salvation in order to be saved and born again. We all are going to struggle from time to time because we have to overpower our flesh daily. But as long as we keep our hearts and minds on Christ, he will sustain us through it all.

Proverbs 18:11: "A human spirit can endure in sickness, but a crushed spirit who can bear?"

Proverbs 18:14: "A spirit of a man will sustain his infirmity but a wounded spirit who can bear?"

These verses give us knowledge that the condition of our spirits is very important. Whatever we face will be dealt with according to our spirit's condition. If our spirit is weak, then we will have a weak resolution. If our spirit is strong and built on the word of God, then we will operate in power from Jesus. We will not be moved by any old thing that comes up against us because we know that we are victorious. No matter what comes at us, we know who we are, and we know who we belong to. It does not change the word of God.

To sustain is to support physically or mentally. We have to remember that we wrestle not against flesh and blood, but with spirits from dark places. We are not perfect, but we are made perfect in God's image. The bible even tells us that when we fall we have to get back up because God knew that we would sometimes fall. Jesus got up from the grave on the third day from death, so that was proof to me that he got up so that we could get up from anything that may have knocked us down or caused us to get unstable during our walk with God.

Proverbs 24:17 says: "For though a righteous man falleth seven times, they rise again, but the wicked stumble when calamity strikes."

Calamity is an event causing offense or distress; a disaster.

During your life, you will experience times when things will happen that are set up to make you fall apart, but when you are saved, you will not fall apart because you know who you belong to and you know that Jesus will sustain you. You know that whatever comes up against you had to have permission from God to even occur, so with that being said, if God allowed it, then he knows that you have the tools to defeat it. He has given us authority; we have to use it.

Receiving salvation stops all of the things that the enemy plans for you from succeeding. The weapon may form, but it will not prosper.

It doesn't matter what the enemy tries or which way he will come because you are shielded all the way around, and he won't be able to win at all. Your faith determines how quick the process will be. Some things may seem like they are not fair, but if it is God's will, then it will all work out for the good.

I can remember going through things over and over again and then, I finally realized that God had given me weapons which were prayer, dominion, boldness, and authority, and I started commanding things to move as well as things to come forth in Jesus's name.

Once I did that, I activated my faith and started believing that God was in control and everything that he promised was going to take place. I started believing that it didn't matter what I saw or what my circumstances seemed like. What mattered was what I believed, and my beliefs were way more powerful and positive than what I'd seen. There were days that I had no food and my assistance for food stamps had been cut off because they said that I had exceeded the amount for eligibility. I didn't worry; not one day. I just prayed and thanked the Lord in advance for supplying my household's needs. I touched my fridge every day and I said, "Thank you Lord for providing the meals that my family needs to survive." There were times when folks brought food, gave me money, or called me about references that were giving food assistance. These people had no clue what my circumstances were. They were just doing what the Lord had commanded them to do, and they were being obedient while being used as willing vessels.

They had no clue what my fridge was looking like, and they had no clue what my family's needs were, or the way that I was living; from check to check. Not being able to pay my bills on time or having what I needed. I studied poverty and I learned that poverty is a mindset. Once I realized that, I asked the Lord to renew my mind. I started to look at my situation differently. I didn't look like what I was going through anymore. I walked with my head held high and I didn't present myself as a person of poverty. I knew who God created me to be and my condition didn't define my destiny. Poverty has potential, and until you tap into who you truly are in Christ, you will remain stagnate and dealing with things that are not acceptable in Jesus's eyes. I had to remember that poverty is not the condition, but it is just the way that the enemy has tricked your mind into thinking that you have less than God has provided. I had to start giving back to Christ exactly what I was in need of because if God provides, then he had given me what I needed to make it. I just had to use what I had and ask God where I needed to sow it. I had to plant the little that I was blessed with so that it could grow when harvest season showed up. I needed food, so I would feed who I could with what I had. I needed love, so I spread love as much as I could. I needed someone to help me and lead me in the right direction, so I made sure that I was a great leader to everyone that God had assigned me to. I didn't worry about lack because the bible says that, "We are the lenders and not the borrowers"(Deuteronomy 28:12-13). "We have to give to receive" (Luke 6:38).

I knew that fear was not a factor. I couldn't be saved when things were going right and then get unsaved when things were going wrong. Once I was saved, I was saved. There was no demon in hell that could undo that because they didn't save me in the first place. The only person that could undo things was Jesus because he did it all. He made a way for me to walk through doors that no man could open, and he closed doors behind me that needed to come to an end. I am so thankful for salvation today. This was the second step that I took on my Journey of following Christ. I didn't know what to do to be saved, and the bible helped me by being a map to eternal life. The only thing that I had to do was follow the instructions.

Romans 10: 9,10: "That if thou shall confess with thy mouth the Lord Jesus, and shalt believe in thine heart that God hath raised him from the dead, thou shalt be saved."
10 "For with the heart, man believeth unto righteousness; and with the mouth confession is made unto salvation."

Confession is the way to salvation. I had to not only believe in my heart what the bible says concerning Jesus, but I had to confess it. This showed me that a lot of things that I believed had to be confessed because if I confessed with my mouth that Jesus died on the cross and rose from the dead and I was saved, then I could confess anything over my life in Jesus's name and it was so as well.
This chapter is the step that you have to take before you go any

further in your journey of building God's Kingdom. You cannot be successful in the kingdom if you are not first saved from the danger of sin and born again with the holy spirit operating through you. Salvation is a must!

TRANSFORMATION

Transformation is a thorough or dramatic change in form or appearance.

Step 3 was a step that allowed me to see a difference in myself. I was able to have an outer body experience and see the things that I needed to change. I thought that I had it all together because of salvation, but I still needed to be transformed. I worried a lot about how other people saw me and what others had to say about my life, but I never really took a look in the mirror and examined myself. I spent a lot of time trying to please others and making sure that their lives were straight. Meanwhile, my first ministry, which was my household, was falling apart. Before I could help anyone else, I had to help myself. By the time my day was over, I was so tired and worn out from everyone else's problems that I had no strength to tend to my kids. They would ask me to help with homework, talk about how their day was, or just need the nurturing from a parent to a child. I must admit, I look back now and I had put my first and most important ministry on the back burner. I had put my home as last on the list. I received salvation and I was on fire for the Lord. All I wanted to do was work for the Lord. I wanted to reach every soul that I possibly could.

I was tired of the life that I was living, and I wanted everything that God had for me. I went through enough in my life and I wanted the Lord to change me. After a while, I realized that the Lord could assist me with my change, but my nature and character had to line up with Jesus. Making changes involves work done by yourself along with the help of our savior. I can refer back to what I mentioned in Step 2 concerning faith and how without works it is dead. We can't just pray and ask Jesus for things and expect him to just give it to us without teaching us how to work for it. Jesus trains us, the same way he teaches us to train our children. Training is teaching us in a way that we will never forget. In order to be able to receive the proper training , I had to be willing to sacrifice some things. Nothing in life is free. Not even us as human beings. We were bought with a price and there is nothing that compares to the price that Jesus payed for us to live. We don't deserve grace, but he gives us grace, and he also helps us to give it to others ,even when they don't deserve it. He also gives us victory.   If we want victory out of certain situations, we must first surrender because the victory is our's once we surrender. I learned in the word of God   that having   victory is basically remaining faithful, no matter what it looks like. Not being moved by things that are set up by the enemy to discourage you. Victory is having joy because you know that God is on the throne.   I couldn't go through certain obstacles without Jesus, so I had to acknowledge that God is God and he is the head of my life. I made up my mind that I believed that Jesus is God's son and there was no way at all that I could get to God except through him. I asked for forgiveness and I had to forgive others, because if i didn't then he would not forgive me.

Matthew 6:15: "But if you do not forgive others their sins, your father will not forgive your sins."

I started looking at myself and the way that I was dressing, talking, and carrying myself. I was conformed to the ways of the world.

To be conformed is to be similar in form or type; agree. To correspond to, be consistent with ,measure up to, or tally with.

I was keeping up with the styles and the latest things that were out in the world. I had to meditate on the word of God in order to change. The more I read the word, the more I felt separated from the world. I started conforming to the word of God. I had been praying for a transformation to take place, and I didn't want to go any longer feeling like I was on both sides of the fence. My heart had changed, but my outer appearance was looking just like the world, and my mind was still thinking carnal every now and then. A carnal mind is a mind that is of the flesh; denoting human nature.

Romans 8:7: "Because the mind set on flesh is hostile toward

God; for it does not subject itself to the law of God, for it is not even able to do so.

God had given me a gift to be creative in my own way and it was a way that others would ask," where did you get that from? or how did you get that idea"? I can remember several people telling me, "Tonya, you look like a queen." I felt like a queen when I had my mind made up to be confident and walk in it. God had spoken to me concerning my identity in him and I didn't have to carry myself any kind of way. I had to walk like the woman of God that he had called me to be. Other people's lives were in my hands and I had to be obedient and submit to my assignment from God. God wanted to use me 100% as a willing vessel so that people would see Christ in me; not Tonya. God called me to be a CEO of a group 'WOMEN OF VIRTUE." It was going to be impossible to lead a group without transformation taking place in my life first. Before I could lead, I had to show God that I was a great follower. I had to follow the instructions that God had sent through my spiritual leader. I had a problem with submitting for a while, and that is why the Lord did not open doors for me in certain areas. I was so caught up in the world and I was guilty of seeing people and things for what they were presenting, instead of who or what God created them to be. My mind definitely needed to be renewed and transformed.

Romans 12:2 says: Do not be conformed to this world, but be transformed by the renewal of your mind, that by testing you may discern what is the will of God. What is good and acceptable and perfect."

I couldn't lead women and teach them to be virtuous without being set free from the ways of the world. The mission that God had created me for required me to be serious, but loving and bold for Christ. I had to be renewed in my mind, because in order to work with different personalities or natures I had to have a new mind set. My mission involved being flexible and getting rid of my old ways of thinking or handling things certain ways. All old things had to pass away. I could not receive the new things that God had for me until I did away with my past first. There is no way that the old can live with the new. It's either one or the other.

2 Corinthians 5:17: "Therefore, if anyone is in Christ, he is a new creation. The old has passed away; behold the new has come.

To be virtuous is to have or show high moral standards; to be righteous, good, pure, high minded, and upright.

I studied more about being virtuous in Proverbs 31. This chapter explained exactly what God expected from the women.

Proverbs 11:13: "The integrity of the upright will guide them, but the crookedness of the treacherous will destroy them."

I found my mind to be completely cluttered, so I had to get rid of some of the data that was just sitting there taking up space and reminding me of failure. I can remember riding home one day and God showing me myself compared to a vehicle.

I was needing an oil change because the oil that I had flowing was old from my past. I needed my headlights replaced because there were times that I couldn't see ahead of me or I thought that I saw something that didn't exist. I was looking with the carnal eyes and things were not the way that God wanted me to view them. My transmission was slipping. There were days that I didn't even know what gear I was in. I would start off fast and all of a sudden, I would find myself stuck. My spirit was all jacked up. I can imagine myself feeling stranded and broken down just like a vehicle that had a flat with no spare tire in the trunk. I had no foundation, so I had nothing that could hold me up when I was falling. My spirit was supposed to sustain me but, how? It wasn't even built up strong enough to block those things that were attacking me or better yet, deal with them. My rear view mirrors were bigger than my wind shield. All I could see was the things from my past and how much I had failed in life. I was focusing on all of the people who had let me down and had spoken negative words over me. I focused on the different ministries, friends, relatives, and jobs that were not successful for me because that was all that I could see in the rear view. Bad relationships, cancelled engagements, hurt, abandonment, resentment, pain, fake love, fake what's up's, fake hugs, and favors that really were done just to expose what I was lacking at the time. I had to replace my front wind shield so that I could get a better view on life. I needed God to remove the vail. Things were so small, but it was the little things that God wanted me to address in my life. The little things are what caused the things in my rearview to look so big because they were not brought to God and left there for him to work out.

Example:

*Praying for my enemies.

*Praying and waiting on God to give me a for sure answer before

I joined ministries, groups, organizations, jobs, or churches.

*Praying for God to work on myself before I pray for him to work on my husband.

*Praying for God to show me who to receive from because not everyone's intentions were to really bless me or see me grow spiritually.

*Praying for God to reveal my purpose, because whatever it was, it had my career tied up in it as well.

*Praying for my family instead of getting upset when they did things that bothered me.

There was a lot ahead of me that I had to prepare and pray about. Prayer made the things in my rear view mirror start to disappear because they started to be irrelevant in my walk for Christ. They were now in God's hands and my focus was to stick to the mission and continue to pray as God works on the thing that I had no control over.

Still comparing myself to a vehicle, I realized my tail lights were out. I expected people to follow me but they didn't know which way I was going. I had no signals to warn them of any turns. Whenever I stopped on breaks suddenly, they would crash right into the back of me because there was never a warning. I was stopping and starting back up every time the devil attacked me. I was stopping more frequently than before because I was so confused about which way I was going. I thought I had lost my mind! I couldn't lead anyone when I didn't even know the directions myself. I looked down to check my GPS and I had it, but it wasn't activated. It was the word of God. I carried my bible with me, but I only opened it when I was in service. The GPS could not direct me if I barely opened it or followed directions. I didn't know what chapter or scripture to turn to because I never programed it in my mind. It wasn't connected to me to remind me where to go whenever I made a wrong turn or was stuck at a dead end. My brakes went out after a while. I had careless accidents; running into people that were not even connected to my destiny. I had been places where I wasn't supposed to be and I didn't have the grace for the territory in those areas. I needed to be balanced! Not being grounded and rooted in the word caused me to be all over the road and that brought a lot of unnecessary attention to me. Exposing myself to everyone that said I would fail and allowing them to see how bad I was struggling with my mind.

The body of my vehicle (my outside appearance) looked like I was in good shape, but I needed to be transformed and renewed. I needed a full-service job.

I prayed so hard and long for Jesus to help me with transformation because I didn't want to look like I was running effectively, but feel like I was breaking down. Busy doing nothing, I needed Jesus to take all of my salvaged parts out and give me a new start. I started studying more because I always wanted to be so anointed. I learned that the anointing destroys the yokes but without knowledge, we are destroyed and gone into captivity. The bible also speaks about the Lord rejecting us and forgetting our children because we reject the knowledge that we need.

Hosea 4:6: "My people are thou shalt be no priest to me: seeing thou hast forgotten the law of thy God, I will also forget thy children."

Isaiah: 5:13: "Therefore, my people are gone into captivity, because they have no knowledge :and their honorable men are famished, and their multitude dried up with thirst."

Captivity is the condition of being imprisoned or confined; incarceration, detention, or internment.

Lack of knowledge will leave you feeling like you are locked up or slaved. I had to be transformed and one way of doing that was to gain knowledge of the word of God. Having the knowledge of the word helped me when it came to my confidence. I was bolder and I felt more secure about what I was talking about when it came to spreading the gospel. My faith was strengthened because of knowledge and I watched myself transform into a person who walked boldly and with a high self-esteem; knowing that what God says for my life was not a lie and his word was my foundation. I studied the word of God every chance that presented itself and I asked the Lord to give me revelations on what I was reading so that I could understand what the word was teaching. I came across an article one day that mentioned a few steps to help with transformation, so I thought that it would be good to share with the readers of this book.

Here are a few things that I studied and practiced so that transformation could take place.

1) Develop positive thinking.

This was the first keystone habit that helped me form the other important habits. Positive thinking by itself does not lead to success, but goes a long way and it motivates you to do the other things that are required.

2)Exercise

Exercising made me feel better about myself and it was showing God that I respected my temple more. It helped me relieve so much stress. Exercising reinforced positive thinking habits because I had to think positive in order to sustain exercise. Exercising also gave me time to think things over and it led to a better mental- well being because there were days that I was overwhelmed and I thought that I was going to lose my mind.

3)Single-Tasking

This is the opposite of multi-tasking. The more that I practiced this, the more I felt at peace about my work that I was doing as well as my assignments that God was instructing me to do. I started doing one thing at a time verses how I was doing hundreds of things at the same time before. I was able to complete things and get things done in order. When I started writing this book, I was doing five different things at one time. By the time that I had sat down to type, my words were all over the place because my mind was all over the place. It's hard to achieve important things when you are constantly switching up tasks and distracted by other "urgent things." You have to be stable and know how to balance. I wasn't stable at all, so this practice really helped me.

4)Focus on one goal

This is similar to Step 3. It was very difficult at first because I am a woman who has many goals and all of them are important to me. I had to make a list and categorize long term and short term because I had to reach one goal at a time. Just like the single -tasking it was becoming difficult trying to do many things at one time. Even though God has blessed me to be able to do many things, there were some things that required my undivided attention. Some things needed to be in my priority stack and some could wait. I was able to reach most of my goals once I learned to focus on one at a time.

5)Eliminate the non -essential

To do this, first I had to identify what was essential. These were the things that were most important to me; the things that I loved the most.

Then I had to eliminate everything else because there was no need in working on things that I didn't really care about. Those things were just distractions and they were causing delays. Eliminating the non-essential helped me simplify things in my life and it made more space for the things that were essential. This was like cleaning out my closet and getting rid of the clothes or shoes that I don't wear. It was always better for me to see what I had and most of the time I had clothes with tags on them, but I couldn't see them for all of the non-essential stuff. This project helped me with a lot of things in my life like emails, presentations, studying, budgeting, planning, and communication.

6) Kindness

Believe it or not, kindness had to become a habit in order to be transformed. All of the steps helped me with transformation, but this one was very important because I had to be more like Jesus. I had to give the same grace to folks that God gave me. Even though most people didn't deserve it, I still had to display Jesus. I started feeling better about myself and people started reacting differently to me. They started treating me better because I was treating people how I expected to be treated; not how they treated me. Trust me, I know just about every one of my enemies because the Holy ghost does not leave me ignorant. I can also hear the persecution in the spirit sometimes during my meditation. God lets me know what to pray for as well as to stay alert, but I still had to be kind to them because it is the will of God. Being kind to those people was part of my test that opened doors for me to move to the next level. It was like graduation to me. Each time that I was kind to someone that was mean to me, I was able to see if I was really spiritually matured. When I used to see these people, I used to smile and say, "God bless." Some people look at blessings like something good is always happening in someone's life, but blessings come in so many different forms. Being chastised is a blessing. Correction is also a blessing because it causes people to change. I was convicted of things that I did wrong in the past and going to jail ended up being a blessing to me.

For example, when I was younger, I got into some trouble because I was hard headed. I went to jail for fighting. Till this day, I look back and I thank God for that being a blessing. Yes, a blessing! If I didn't go to jail back then, I may have been dead or in jail today. God opened up my eyes to reality a long time ago and it was a blessing in a form of a punishment. I used to think that God was mad at me for doing wrong things, but he wasn't mad. He was just allowing me to deal with consequences to my actions. The same way that we are with our children.

Being kind is not easy at all, but practice makes you better. Now, I have no problem with being kind to any one that hurts me or speaks down on me because God is the ruler and he makes the decisions for all of our lives . Whatever we do behind someone else's back is always done RIGHT IN FRONT OF GOD'S FACE!! Kindness can be considered a goal and the more you focus on reaching it, the more you will see yourself getting better at it.

7) Daily Routine

Creating a daily routine for myself made a big difference in my life. I had to develop a routine for when I woke up, for when I went to work , for when I finished my work day ,and for the end of my evening until I went to bed. Having a routine helped me make sure that I had everything done that was planned for that day. It helped me meet deadlines and I didn't miss appointments. My life had become a schedule instead of just being open to any and everything. When I was asked to engage, attend certain events, or help with different things, I had to check my calendar first. I had to get me a secretary to help me so now my organizational and time management skills were better. I can count on one hand how many times that I may have been late in one year. I was punctual, and learning to be a virtuous woman helped me value my time more.

8) Prayer Life

I saved the best for last. "My Prayer Life " .

I can remember watching the movie "War Room." I was so impressed and I had just started getting my prayer life on point. I was praying three, sometimes four times a day and I was meditating on and in God to hear him talk back to me concerning my life. I worshipped God in my prayer time. I always told him how much I adored him and magnified him. I asked God to fill me up with an anointing that would destroy yokes that the enemy thought he was going to keep connected. I fasted, and prayed for weeks at a time, praying in the Holy ghost.

My mentor and spiritual father, Prophet Kuassi told us in bible study that praying in tongues helped build our spirits. He showed us in the bible in Jude 1:20: "But ye, beloved building up yourselves on your most Holy faith, praying in the Holy ghost."

Praying in tongues allowed my spirit to pray for me. I had some days when I didn't know what to pray for because there was so much coming at me at once, but when I started praying in the holy ghost, my spirit was letting God know what I needed to make it through. My spirit knew what to pray for because the bible tells us that we do not know ourselves.

Romans 8:26: "Likewise, the spirit helps us in our weakness. For we do not know what to pray for as we ought , but the spirit himself intercedes for us with groanings too deep for words."

I pray that this chapter of Transformation will help you and you will get a better understanding of changing yourself instead of focusing on changing others first. There is more to transformation besides your outer appearance. Your attitude, nature, and character play very important roles in transforming. You cannot say that you are a display of Christ and perform like Satan. Get rid of the old things that are not working for you to get closer to your destiny. The things that are hindering you from perusing your purpose and operating in your full potential for the kingdom of God. Your purpose is important because your life depends on it. You cannot be who God wants you to be until you transform and walk in your purpose.

ACCEPTING, EXPECTING & RECEIVING

This was a tough subject to write about because it is so hard for folks to accept things that they cannot change and still expect things to turn out just fine. I went through a season in my life where folks were always saying, "God will work it out or in due time you will reap the harvest." I also was told, "He won't put any more on you than you can bear, or God has not forgotten you." Boy, did I get tired of hearing these things and I was not seeing anything happen like God said. I read these same things in the bible and they were said to be true, but things were just not happening for me like I wanted them to. I found myself depressed, stressed out, and giving up on God. I had thoughts of suicide and I just wanted to run away from the world. Nobody understood how I felt because I thought that once I was transformed, I didn't have to worry about setbacks or struggles any more. I figured that because I have a new mindset now, my thinking wasn't gonna be negative and things would not feel the same. Well, I was wrong. I got attacked even more because now the devil really wanted my soul. He did not want to let me go that easy. I had conquered so many things, so he started digging up the same tricks, but he switched up people and places. The enemy knew that I had conquered some areas in my life and even though I still was faced with obstacles my experiences made them easier to push through them. There was a few things that I still struggled with and the enemy knew that they were Accepting, Expecting, and Receiving.

There were some things in my life that God wanted me to go through because in order for me to help or testify to others, I had to experience some things myself. I had to accept that I couldn't go to certain places anymore, I couldn't indulge in certain activities or conversations (no matter how exciting they seemed).

I had to accept the fact that I was going to be single for a few years with no sex, no dating, no lusting, and no commitments until I engaged into the word of God and married Jesus. My only commitment for a while was to Jesus and him only. I had to accept that God is jealous and he wants all of me; not half. I can remember talking to Jesus and I asked him, "Why is it that I pray, but nothing happens like it happens for others?" Jesus told me that I get exactly what I offer. It's not about receiving, but it is about giving and expecting. I was giving 90% to God because I wanted to hold on to that small piece of fornication in my spirit. A man is gifted with a sense of security and it is something about a man that makes you feel like everything is gonna be ok. I didn't walk around lusting about every man that I laid eyes on because I do know that having sexual desires and you're not married is a sin; especially if it's not for your husband. I had to be delivered from a lusting spirit. I had to accept the fact that I would not be with a man until I experienced the true love of Jesus. Not only did I have to experience real love , but I had to exhibit it as well. I had to show Jesus that I love him as much as he loves me. I had days that I felt like I would never come close to that type of love (Agape love) because I didn't think that I was capable of loving Jesus the way that he loves me. What mattered was that I strived for it each and every day. I had to accept the fact that God created me to care for people no matter how they treated me. I cared for elderly people, babies, homeless people, prostitutes, drug addicts, alcoholics, friends that weren't really friends, family that preyed on me instead of praying for me, and the list goes on. I even mentored children from kindergarten up to women that were 75-years-old. I funded churches that didn't want me around and I supplied care packages for people that didn't appreciate my help, but that was something that I had to accept. Having to accept things that you do not agree with can be tough sometimes. I realized that I didn't have to agree with everything that took place, but I had to accept the fact that some things just happen because they are in God's will. The things that happen are not to harm us but to prosper us. (Jeremiah 29:11)

Accepting is the consent to receive, take, gain, or obtain.

When you accept something, you believe or come to recognize its purpose . Accepting is giving credence to; trust.

Once I accepted Jesus Christ as my savior, I accepted every choice that was made concerning my life. The only question that I had was " Which way do you want me to go Lord, or when?"

I understood that if I believed that Jesus had rose from the dead, then I had to also believe everything else that the bible stated concerning him. I couldn't accept the fact that he is the son of God but not accept the fact that the wages of sin are death. I learned a lot about myself once I started accepting what was written about my journey. Accepting was an act of surrendering for me. It let God know that whatever he said, I was gonna follow it, and whatever he told me to do was fine with me because I agreed to it and I trusted him. Your belief has a lot to do with accepting and trusting. You will not accept whatever you do not believe. My beliefs shifted recently. I believed in God, but I had to trust him in order to see a reaction. Whatever you believe determines the way you will live. I started trusting God no matter what I was going through. No matter what the situation looked like; I still praised the Lord because I knew that his word explained the plans that he had for my life.

The Lord taught me how to receive as well. When you receive something, you are given, presented, or payed something.

One thing that I learned about receiving is that you have to do something first before you receive. It's not always material or physical when you give, but most of the time it's spiritual. In the bible, there were several times that something had to take place before a blessing, gift, or reward came. for example:

Matthew 6:33: "But seek ye first the kingdom of God and his righteousness, and all these things will be added to you."

2 Corinthians 9:6: The point is this: "Whoever sows sparingly will also reap sparingly, and whoever sows bountifully will also reap bountifully."

Then there is the greatest verse that always represents giving to receive and it is John 3:16: " For God so loved the world that he gave his only begotten son, that whoever believes in him should not perish but have eternal life."

Even God gave something so that we could receive something. So therefore He should receive our souls, our salvation, and our willingness to let Christ live in us. Receiving always involves giving first. It takes an action from ourselves in order to get a reaction that we are expecting from God.

Expecting means to regard something as likely to happen.

Jeremiah 29:11 is one of my favorite verses: "For I know the plans I have for you, declares the Lord, plans for welfare and not for evil, to give you a future and hope."

A plan is an intention or decision about what one is going to do; intent, objection, goal, target, aim. To decide on or arrange in advance

God made plans way before we were born for us to live a prosperous life.

Welfare means the health, happiness, and fortunes of a person or group. It is the well-being, comfort, security, safety, protection, prosperity, success, and fortune.

This basically explains that God's plans are not for us to live in poverty or have less than we need. If we are living any other way than the word of God says that we should, then it is not God's fault because that is not his plans for our lives. I live by this verse (Jeremiah 29:11) whenever I feel myself beginning to worry about certain things like bills, health, or security. I have to remind myself that God's plans are different from my circumstances and my thoughts. The word of God gives me hope and it teaches me to expect in a different way.

The Lord had spoken to me one day concerning my expectations. An expectation is a strong belief that something will happen or be the case in the future. When something is planned, it is not planned because it has already happened, it is planned because you expect it to happen. When you plan ,you have hope for things falling through successfully the way that you planned for them to. The Lord was showing me how I shower every night after work and I get in the bed; saying my prayers and expecting to wake up the next day to head to work. The reason the Lord knew that I expected to wake up is because I had always had my clothes laid out for the next day. I had " planned" my next day ahead of time. My expectations were high concerning waking up. I didn't have a doubt in my mind that I was not going to be at work the next day. That is the same way that the Lord wants us to be about the word of God. The Lord wants us to be expecting great things to take place in our lives because he says in his word that it is his plans for us to live prosperous. I was often praying prayers, but I wasn't expecting anything. The more that I studied the word, I seen that I had to build my faith up to a level where I didn't just read the word, but I saw the word manifesting in my life because of my beliefs and expectations. I couldn't see these certain things with my physical eyes. I had to see them in the spirit. Everything that the Lord says is true and it comes to pass, but we have to have expectations along with faith; knowing that God is gonna do just what he said in his word. Your expectations have so much to do with what you believe. When you believe that God is gonna work it out, then you don't get worried, you don't stress, you don't waver. You just stand firm and wait on God to do exactly what he said in his word. The truth is, God has already done it. We are just waiting on the manifestation of it. I have learned that my beliefs can make something happen right now that may have been meant to happen next week or next year. The way that I operate in faith will determine how quick I receive what I am expecting.

When my expectations changed, I was no longer surprised about the things that God was doing in my life. The bible said that these things would take place, so I believed it, and I waited on them to happen. I can remember when my hours were cut at work. I didn't panic at all. I started praising the Lord for my new job because I already knew that he had worked it out. When I started on my new job, I was so grateful, but it was like I was already there because I had been praising the Lord way before I got the job. I expected the Lord to bless me and provide for me. It states in the bible that the Lord is Jehovah -Jireh (Yaweh-yireh); our provider. I knew that he would not leave me stranded or stuck in the worst way.

I learned to be surmised. I had to believe in my heart that the word was true without having any evidence to confirm it. My evidence was the life that I lived and the grace that was on it. I must say that I am very blessed to have been through what I've been through and still be here to share my story. The evidence that I had was the Holy spirit. The Holy spirit was always there to lead me in the right direction. As long as I had it living inside of me, there was no question about living like Christ.

I went through things that no one could even imagine. I can remember folks telling me: "Girl, I don't think I could walk in your shoes," or "Girl, there must be a major calling on your life."

The truth is, it doesn't really matter what the calling is on your life because we are all called to build God's kingdom. Once we agree to participate in that, we basically have to take up our crosses and walk. We are going to get hit by so many things because of the choices that we made to allow Jesus to abide within us. The condition of your spirit is what will determine if you can withstand the attack or not. The more I studied the bible and built a stronger relationship with God, the more the attacks felt like baby licks. They got lighter. I had to learn that the devil is not after us, he is after the spirit in us. The Holy spirit helps us and it warns us of the tricks that the devil plans against our destiny. That is why it is so important that we have the Holy spirit living in us. Without it, we are truly lost.

I pray that this chapter of accepting, receiving, and expecting has blessed you. Learn to receive the Holy spirit and trust God to make decisions for your life. It will help you when you are faced with situations that are hard to accept, but right for your destiny. This step helped me to accept the fact that I am extraordinary and I am not going to be able to have or do what others do because God has chosen me to take a different route.

HUMILITY

Humility is a modest or low view of one's own importance; humbleness.

Humility involves being modest or meek. Here are a few steps that helped me while practicing humility.

1) Avoid taking credit: There were times when I used to make progress in something and I found myself bragging, saying, "I did it, I did it!" I had to really step back and realize that I did nothing; God did it.

2) Praise others for their good deeds or accomplishments: Even though I was struggling with somethings, I didn't let that stop me from congratulating others for their success. I probably didn't get the job, but I was happy for the people that did get it.

3) Help others succeed: I was blessed to be able to walk in certain places in my life without a high school Diploma or GED. I have God's favor all over me and I was connected to some people that had the answers that I needed. Not only that; they made things much easier for me also. God's grace opened up doors as well. When I met people that needed help and direction, I helped them and turned them on to some of my connections. I didn't withhold information that could help someone else go up the ladder. I reached out to the people that were once where I was and I lifted them up.

4) Admit your mistakes or when you're wrong: A lot of times in the past, I knew that I was wrong, but I wouldn't dare say it. Practicing humility made it so much easier for me to admit when I was wrong. I was more passionate about other's feelings, and I did

not want to walk around acting like I was right when I wasn't. I didn't mind correction or going back to make things right. My character was built up more whenever I was able to admit when I was wrong. It showed others that I was not always right and I could receive correction whenever I wasn't. (correction is love). It's hard to deal with people that can't receive, especially when they are wrong. They can easily ship out but it is hard for them to take in. They need to check their shipping and receiving department . In order for anything to run well in your life you must have both departments running effectively. Take in as much as you dish out and you will more than likely find yourself becoming slow to speak. You will realize that your not so perfect after all and you have some things that you could be working on to better yourself instead of judging others.

5) Learn from others: I was open to new ideas and I didn't mind doing things different from the ways that I had done them for so long. Even though the ways that I had things set up may have been working for me, I did not let that stop me from learning new things. I got in touch with my creative side and I opened up my mind to new things and new people.

6) Go last instead of always wanting to be first: Matthew 20:16: "So the last will be first and the first will be last." This verse says a lot and it helped me in my life when I had issues with always wanting to be recognized or in the front. I no longer fight to be recognized because God is going to bless me no matter what. I don't have to fight for a platform because the platform will send for me when God is ready for me to be heard. There are people that may have been in position for 20 years or better, but that did not mean anything in God's eyes. God will bless me the same according to my humility. Just because I haven't been studying the bible for a long time, that does not take away from who God says that I am and where he plans for me to be in this season. People get so caught up in numbers and they forget about God. God can turn a 1 into 100 quick! He is God!

7) Serve someone: In order to please God, you must be his servant. In order to be a servant, you must serve. I remember wanting to be a manager at Fire House Subs and I had to first be a regular employee. I had to experience all of the hard jobs that didn't seem so fun before I could move up. I had to mop floors, clean toilets, and sometimes slice meat for hours. I look back now and I

see how I had to serve first before I could be served as a manager or leader. Once I moved up to manager; I was giving orders and now I had people serving me. I didn't have to work so hard anymore but, I had to start out cleaning the bathrooms or vacuuming the floor before I could even move up to the position.

I also had to serve in God's house and make things easier on my pastor. There were times that he didn't have to ask me. The holy spirit had given me instructions, so I just did it. I even made care packages for the community. I went around looking for people that I could help and make a difference in their lives. The smile on their faces made my day. I always asked God to send me to people that I could serve with the love of Jesus. It was my passion to help others.

The only way to be humble is to be humbled. It seems difficult, but it can be done and it allows doors to open for you instead of you trying to open them yourself. When you are humbled, there is nothing that anyone will not discuss with you or ask you for your help in, because your spirit is easy and you are not always on the edge. Folks usually don't care to work with or never the less talk to people that think that they know everything or that it is all about them. The Lord elevates you when you put yourself in a place that you make it known that you are nothing without him.

2 Chronicles 7:14 says, "If my people, who are called by my name ,will humble themselves and pray and seek my face and turn from their wicked ways, then I will hear from heaven , and I will forgive their sin and will heal their land. "

This verse says a lot. If we humble ourselves, Jesus will heal our land. This goes back to the last chapter when I said "You must first do something in order for God to do something. Humility is part of our instructions for healing. A lot of times we expect God to do so much; especially heal us, but we fail to do what the word instructs us to do. If the instructions were not important, then the bible would not tell us to do them. I've met so many people in my lifetime that talk about humility, but are far from humble. People that focus more on the gifts and the anointing instead of getting the knowledge of God inside of them. The bible states in Romans 11:29: "For the gifts and calling of God are without repentance."

The gifts come regardless, without repentance, but you have to be humble enough to allow the gift to be effective. It is possible to operate in a gift and not be effective or not see any changes. This happens because a demon can't cast out another demon. How are you gonna lay hands on someone that needs to humble themselves when you have the same issue? How can you pray for a spirit of sexual immorality to leave when you have an issue with pornography or fornication? It's like being a hypocrite. The demon that you are trying to cast out is laughing at you because you both are familiar or related; of the same kind. You can't make corrections if you are not willing to be corrected. I have met some people that are ok as long as they are the ones doing the correcting and making changes, but as soon as someone else corrects them, it's a problem.

As I learned to humble my spirit, I literally went and found every individual that claimed to have had a problem with me or said that I had wronged them. I reached out to old friends; even enemies, and I tried to make things right with them. I had some situations that didn't work out so well because folks are not delivered from that spirit that holds on to the past. (grudges) But it's ok because I had to get that bad blood off of my hands. I also had some folks that were humble enough to receive a genuine apology and agree to move on in life in Jesus name. When I became more humble, I found myself apologizing for things that I was not wrong about and taking action or making the first move to make things right. God is so awesome! When you are humble, you don't really care about what people think. All you care about is what God thinks about the life that you are living. When I became humble, I realized that I no longer had to talk loud or act out of character to get my point across. The bible says to give a gentle answer to turn away wrath.

Proverbs 15:1: "A gentle answer turns away wrath, but a harsh word stirs up anger."

Being Humble is beneficial to your life:

1) God gives FAVOR. Proverbs 3:34

2) The reward of humility and the reverent and worshipful fear of the Lord is RICHES and HONOR and LIFE. Proverbs 22:4

3) When pride comes, then comes disgrace, but with the humble is WISDOM. Proverbs 11:2

Life is so much better with God's gifts. When you humble your spirit, you will be able to experience God's amazing gifts. You will not have Lack of faith in God which comes by focusing more on what we can see instead of who God is. We have to focus on what he has already done and will do if we only ask him. The bible says that "We have not because we ask not."

Some people focus too much on God doing what they pray for instead of focusing on who He is. You have to believe that what you are praying for is already done. No matter what the outcome looks like; you have to remember that He is still God and He has all power in his hands. God is in control of our lives. Sometimes he makes us wait on what we are praying for because timing is important. He also waits on us to practice humility because we cannot have certain things until we are humble enough to receive them. God knows that we will get the "big head" or forget who gave it to us or placed us in the position that we are in today. We will become better than what we were and forget who made us.

Some people don't even pray anymore because they are afraid of being disappointed if they pray and God doesn't answer. So, they fearfully avoid talking to God, but they still expect God to come through for them. I've learned that the problem is that we often compare God's power to our own feelings of powerlessness. We concentrate on weakness too much. The fact that we choose to look inward at our own power causes us to deny God's power, his authority over the darkness that we are dealing with, and his desire to help us enjoy life .

The opposite of humility is PRIDE! Pride gets in the way of our blessings because we have a guard up that says that we don't need anybody, we don't want to hear what nobody has to say, and we have it all figured out on our own because nobody helps us. That is so false! Every day that we wake up, we have help. We do not wake up on our own. We do not put one foot in front of the other on our own. We do not breathe on our own. At any point of the day, we can collapse and fall dead to the floor. We need God all of the time because we literally cannot do ANYTHING without him.

"Pride goes before destruction" A haughty spirit before a fall. (Proverbs 16:18). "Humility goes to the one who overcomes the destruction and the destroyer" (John 1:5).

PRAYERLESSNESS IS A RESULT OF PRIDE! ANSWERED PRAYERS ARE A RESULT OF HUMILITY!

The more that I studied about humility, I came up with questions for myself.

1) How different would my interactions with others be if I only depended on God and learned to honor him?

2) How much more satisfying would my life be if I let God orchestrate a rich and satisfying life instead of trying to create one on my own?

3) How much more fruitful would my decisions be if I waited for and acted on God's wisdom, not my own?

WAITING ON GOD, SHOWS HUMILIITY

Pride does not wait on God. Pride moves ahead of God because it feels like something has to be done now! Pride reacts to fear because it feels like something may go wrong and it can't bear the feeling of embarrassment. You can tell a person who has a lack of faith because it is revealed in the lack of waiting on God. Pride refuses to dwell in God.

"Dwell in me, and I will dwell in you. Just as no branch can bear fruit of itself without abiding in the vine, neither can you bear fruit unless you abide in me." John 15:4

When you are humble, you trust God to lead the way. Humility trusts that God's word is the light to victory. Humility asks God to sustain him/her while they wait. Humility surrenders to God's answers even though it isn't what he/she wants.

In the bible, Jehoshaphat directed his nation to fast and pray when three armies were waiting to take them out. He followed God's very unusual plan:

"You will not have to fight this battle. Take up your positions; STAND FIRM AND SEE THE DELIVERANCE the Lord will give you, Juda and Jerusalem. Do not be afraid; do not be discouraged. Go out to face them tomorrow, and the Lord will be with you." 2 Chronicles 20:17

HUMILITY PRAYS, WAITS, AND OBEYS GOD

Obeying God is a natural result of humbling ourselves before him. Fearing God says that we recognize his instructions for our lives and we understand that we must follow them in order to live victoriously under his protection.

The more that I practiced humility, I became more patient when it came to waiting on God. I can remember going to an interview or even a doctor's appointment, and I would wait patiently in the waiting room or conference room to hear a result or outcome. Nothing or nobody could make me leave because I just had to know the outcome. I had to know if I got the job and I had to know if my physical was healthy. Once I finally received answers after waiting, I felt relieved, and it was all worth the wait. I proved to the employers that I was serious and determined to get the job done. I proved to my doctor that I was serious and concerned about my health.

Waiting on God proves to him that you are serious about the choices that he has made for your life. You are showing God that you trust him and no matter how long it takes, you will not move ahead of him. When you are humble, you pray to God about what the situation is, you wait on him for an answer(no matter how long it takes) , and you obey him when he gives you an answer.

Humility knows that it is not about self at all. It is all about God. Nothing that I do is because of myself. I thought about how I have come so far from who I used to be. God has opened up doors and shown favor and mercy for me. I have grace on my life that gives me the advantages that others do not have. Doors have been opened for me that shouldn't be, due to my past history or decisions. I work a job that I wasn't supposed to qualify for and I live in a place that was supposed to deny me. My humble spirit knows that it was all Jesus! Not by any means was I smart enough or good enough to walk into these places that God had predestined for me. I still struggle with things till this day, but because of my humility, God is able to reach me and save me from all trouble. I'm not too high up in the air on a "high horse" so God can't see about me. I'm not walking around worrying about people hearing or seeing me and what God has done to me during my transformation. I'm not walking around here quoting scripture making people think that I have it all figured out and they don't. I'm not acting as if I can't fall ever again. I am showing gratitude on a daily basis. Putting my pride to death and giving God all of the Glory for everything that he has done through me and for me. I am nothing without God. My humility knows that without the Holy spirit, I am lost, and I know that in order to see God, I must first know Jesus. My humility knows that I have to die and receive Jesus as my savior, while allowing him to live inside of me until my time here on earth is over. I must be able to humble myself enough to deal with correction out of love when my brother or sister is trying to help me. I never know who God is using to send me signs before destruction, and I must never think that anyone is not worthy of helping me.

Practice being humble. It allows God's favor to cover your life. You can go places that people said that you couldn't go, and you will do things that people said you couldn't do. Trust God and let him lead you.

Don't attempt to elevate yourself; that's God's job. When God elevates you, you don't have to worry about disappointment or failing. What God has written for your life, it is so in Jesus' name.

ACTIVATING FAITH

Faith is complete trust or confidence in someone or something. Faith is a strong belief in God or in the doctrines of a religion, based on spiritual apprehension rather than proof.

Hebrews 11:1: "Now faith is the substance of things hoped for, the evidence of things not seen."

Hope is a feeling of expectation and desire for a certain thing to happen. When I studied "the substance of things hoped for," I looked up the word substance. Substance is a particular kind of matter; a physical matter. A matter is an affair or situation under consideration.

So, with a substance being a matter and a matter being a situation, I can explain the first part of this verse to mean that faith is a situation involving expectations because hope is feelings of expectations. Now, the next part of the verse says " The evidence of things not seen." Evidence is the available body of facts or information indicating whether a belief or proposition is true or valid. Evidence is proof, confirmation, or verification of something.

So now, the verse basically explains that Faith is a situation involving expectations and proof or evidence of things that are not seen.

Once I broke the verse down and studied it word for word, I understood what faith is a little better. Growing up, I was always taught that faith was belief and it is. Faith is believing that whatever you are praying about or whatever God says, is going to take place. When you believe something, you trust and you expect something to take place. You can't have faith without expectations. By having expectations, you are telling God that you are waiting patiently and believing because you know that he is going to come through for you. It is not easy to have faith because most people judge situations by what they see and faith cannot be activated by using your eyeballs . You have to use your ears.

The bible says in Romans 10: 17 (NIV) "Consequently, faith comes from hearing the message, and the message is heard through the word about Christ."

Faith comes from hearing the message, meaning the word from God. The verse starts off using the key word, consequently. Consequently means: As a result. A result is an effect or outcome of something. A conclusion or repercussion. So, if this verse says that consequently, faith comes from hearing, it is explaining that there is going to be a result or conclusion out of this. There is no way that you can study or read the word of God and get no results. The word of God changes you and it convicts you. I think about conviction and the times that I went to jail in the past. I have beat myself up all of my life for the charges and convictions that I received. I have been turned away from jobs, homes, and opportunities because of the convictions in my past, so I have been totally against convictions.

But when I found Jesus! I realized that conviction is really good. It is a blessing. I think about the jail cells and the time that I spent at Greenville county detention center. I had time to think about my mistakes and how I should have done things differently. I thought about what I had done wrong and what was not pleasing to God. I look back now and I realize that if I had not gone to jail when I did, I might have gotten in trouble for some things that were worse later on down the years. I was faced with many obstacles and battles. I refused to fall for the devil's tricks because I had a memory of my time spent in jail that was stuck in the back of my mind. I made better decisions because of conviction. I am not saying that it is good to go to jail, but I know that God had his ways of allowing certain things to occur so that I wouldn't continue to follow the same path over and over again. I'm so thankful for the woman that I am today. I overcame plenty of obstacles and the Lord turned them into foot stools; all because of my faith and believing that it all worked for my good.

An obstacle is something that blocks one's way and prevents or hinders progress. A barrier, stumbling block, impediment, handicap, or complication.

Activating faith allows you to move through life free of stress. To activate means to make something active or operative. To initiate, energize, or set in motion.

When you activate something, you are setting it in motion or getting it started up. Whenever you receive a new debit card, you have to call a number and set up new codes, passwords, etc. You get the card ready so that it can receive your benefits or paycheck when it is time. If the card is not activated, then nothing will happen when it's time to reap the benefits. What belongs to you will be there, but you can't put it in motion or get what is yours until it is activated. Faith is the same way. We know that God has given us all a measure of faith so we know that it is there, but if we do not activate it or put it in motion, we cannot operate in it.

Faith is the confidence that says that we hope that it will actually happen ;it gives us assurance about things that we cannot see with our physical eye. What or whom our confidence is in can positively or negatively change our lives. Some people believe in other people(man), some believe in riches, and others believe in themselves. But those who trust only in the Lord will never be put to shame. He never fails!

Faith is not about what we can achieve, it's about what we believe. Sometimes faith is compared to a muscle. A muscle has to be strengthened through exercise. However, faith is not developed through our natural ability. It takes the revelation and grace of God to firmly believe. You have to go through a learning process in order to build your faith.

Here are seven steps that I practiced to help me activate my faith:

1) Feed your faith

Read your bible and begin doing what it tells you to do. You will have a growth spurt in your faith when you follow the word. Psalm 34:8: "O taste and see that the Lord is good: blessed is the man that trusteth in him."

2) Exercise your faith by your actions

Whatever you do in life should be a reflection of what you have learned. John 8:38: says: " I tell the things which I have seen and learned at my father's side, and your actions also reflect what you have heard and learned from your father."

Our greatest desires should be for our deeds to reflect God's instructions.

Psalm 119:5: "Oh, that my actions would consistently reflect your decrees."

3) Speak your faith to make it strong.

2 Corinthians 4:13: "I spoke because I believed."

Your boldness in your faith will open doors of opportunity for you. I didn't think that I would be able to work for a Mentoring Agency because of my past history, but my faith was bold as I applied for the position that God had already ordained me for. I applied knowing that I was called to do this and nothing or nobody was going to be able to get in the way of my calling. I received an email for a training class and I knew that it was the favor of God on my life. I missed out on a lot of opportunities in my life, simply because I didn't activate my faith. I didn't understand the seriousness of confessing things and decreeing that these things would take place in Jesus' name. When I learned how to speak what I needed with a strong belief behind it, that's when I started moving mountains out of my way.

4) Free your faith of negativity

"FEED YOUR FAITH AND STARVE YOUR DOUBTS"-By:Kenneth Hagin

The word negative basically stands for no and it represents doubt or the fact that something is not possible.

James 1:6 : "But let him ask in faith ,nothing wavering , For he that wavereth is like a wave of the sea driven with the wind and tossed."

When doubt leaves your life, you start getting presented with unlimited opportunities. When you have faith without doubting God, you start to walk in a different level in Christ, and you find out that you are able to do all things through Christ.

It states it in Matthew 21:21: "Then Jesus told them, "I tell you the truth, If you have faith and do not doubt ,you can do all things like this and more . You can even say to this mountain," May you be lifted up and thrown into the sea," and it will happen.

How do you get rid of doubt or negativity?

James 4:7: "Submit yourselves therefore to God . Resist the devil and he will flee from you."

Study the word and pray for revelation of it. Study it until something in you "knows that you know" and you start to believe and agree with it. Your hope will start to change to "you know." Faith comes from hearing the word of God. Read your bible. Meditate on it day and night, while believing what it says.

5) Believe the impossible to be possible

Never let fear of things that you don't have knowledge of prevent you from doing what may seem to be impossible because in reality, with God, all things are possible.

Luke 1:37: "For with God nothing is ever impossible and no word from God shall be without power or impossible of fulfillment."

Your belief has to be built on who God is, not what God can do. You have to think of things that he has done already in your life and others. My pastor gave us an example on how God placed a baby in Mary's womb and she was a virgin. They later named him Jesus; the son of God. He also gave an example about the ocean. Look how the water is so deep, the further you go out in it gives you a possibility of drowning and disappearing, but it never comes to dry land and covers the whole earth."

There were times when a storm came and God allowed it in different places on the earth , but he had his reasons. He still controlled all of the water on the earth, only God can do that. Who can protect and feed the animals without them having to work for shelter or food? Who can signal for the birds to fly south in the winter and tell the bears to hibernate? Only God can do these things and they are evidence of his work and who he is.

We have to believe God for who he is and there will be nothing at all that can change our faith because we will know according to what has already taken place.

Your belief determines your actions, and your actions determine your results, but you have to first believe to receive. You can't allow the enemy to fool your mind into thinking that God is limited. He will have you thinking that you can only go so far in life. He is a set up for failure and he specializes in lies and doubtful mindsets.

The enemy placed plenty of stumbling blocks in my path and he planned for me to fail, but I passed every test. After a while, I stopped even giving the devil any credit at all because he doesn't care if it is good or bad; he just wants some credit. I realized that God has his ways of testing us, and he knows how much that we can bare and what is too heavy. The main thing to remember is to keep your faith stronger than what you see visually. If God brought you to it, he will bring you through it. God knows the best things for us and sometimes, he has to let us go through the different experiences in life to build our faith. There were times that I had to get very low and go without somethings in order to know who the real provider was; Jesus! I had put people, places, and things before God. I thought that I had it all figured out on my own. I was never a coward and nothing scared me in the world, but that is where I was wrong. I didn't even fear God. If I did, I would have surrendered to his will a long time ago before now. I had to learn to not just obey God, but submit to his will. You can obey someone without submitting to their will. I found myself doing what God told me to do, only because it was benefiting me, but I didn't follow instructions when I wasn't gaining anything. My faith was only activated when I really needed something to work for me. I thought that I had control over my life.

Once I learned submission and who was in control, my mindset changed and my faith was stronger. My faith was built up off of the word of God, but it was also built up by the things that God had done in my past. The proof that if he did it before, he could do it again. There were times that I needed him and he sent help. He gave his only son to die for us and his son, Jesus, sent the comforter, the Holy spirit to always protect us and live inside of us . Some days I would find myself getting sad or depressed because I felt lonely and I started feeling like no one understood what it was like to walk this walk of living like a holy woman that had to be set apart. I would ball up in my bed and cry myself to sleep, asking the Lord, "Why did you pick me to carry out the gospel or mentor people?" I remember asking the Lord to take the gifts and the calling away and just let me praise him in the back of the crowd, with nobody even knowing my name. My faith waivered every now and again, so I thought I couldn't do it anymore. I was very unstable and my roots needed to be grounded so that I could receive the knowledge that God needed inside of me. I had totally forgotten that I was still human and I was going to fall sometimes. The bible says in Proverbs 24:16: "For though the righteous fall seven times, they rise again, but the wicked stumble when calamity strikes.

Calamity is anything that causes sudden damage or distress. It's better known as a disaster or adversity.

It's not easy being faithful, but it gets easier the more that you read the word of God. The word says that faith comes by hearing and hearing the word of God. I can say that my life became easier, the more I put my faith and trust in God. I stopped worrying about what tomorrow would bring and I refused to dwell on the things of yesterday. I had more folks against me than folks that were for me, but the word also gave me some encouragement concerning that too.

Romans 8:31 says: "What, then, shall we say in response to these things? If God is for us, who can be against us?"

The word does not return void, so I had proof that could sustain me through my weak moments. Not having Faith built up is one of the worst sins that we could ever commit. Our life should be based on pleasing God and living righteous according to the word of God.

Hebrews 11:6 says: "And without faith it is impossible to please God, because anyone who comes to him must believe that he exist and that he rewards those who earnestly seek him."

If you find yourself having a problem with your faith, take it to the manufacturer "Jesus." When you have a car or electronic device, don't you take it to that manufacturer and you let them know what is going on concerning what you have purchased? The reason that you take it back to them is because they created it or put it together so they should be able to assist you with fixing the problem. This is the same way with God. We have to go back to him when our faith is not strong because he knows how to fix us. We have to stay focused on reading the word of God because the scriptures help us and train us to be faithful by hearing the word of God. We have to read the word so that we will be ready for anything that may come our way.

2 Timothy 3:16:17: "All scripture is God -breathed and is useful for teaching, rebuking, correcting, and training in righteousness. (17) so that the man of God may be thoroughly equipped for every good work."

We don't have to worry about things that we do not know while growing in God. We just have to remain faithful and trust the process because if we call on him he will definitely answer and tell us things that we have no knowledge of.

Jeremiah 33:3: "Call to me and I will answer you and tell you great and unsearchable things you do not know."

Activating my faith in this process allowed me to believe the impossible. I believed that anything could happen if I trusted God.

There was no such thing as "maybe or might" in my vocabulary. I knew that God was gonna back me up with his word because I believed him and I also shared my faith with others to show witness to his works, so he had to continue to bless me. We must have faith if we want to please God! When I began to walk as a Woman of God and boldly stepping out in faith, there was nothing that God told me no about. My questions even lined up with the word of God so the Lord made sure that I had everything that I asked for. This step allowed me to get the revelation of what the bible meant by "You have not because you asked not," and" Faith without works is dead."

I often meditate on Ephesians 6:16: "In addition to all this, take up the shield of faith, with which you can extinguish all of the flaming arrows of the evil one."

This verse has given me complete assurance that my faith is what will put out the fires of the enemy. Everything that the enemy tries to send at me will not prosper as long as my faith is activated. I looked up the word extinguish and it said: "To put an end to annihilate, Cause a fire or light to cease to burn or shine."

To terminate, destroy, end, remove, or eliminate. I also thought about a fire extinguisher while reading this verse. A fire extinguisher is used to put out fires. So basically, our faith being activated gives us the ability to cease every attack of the enemy and we can control the heat when things get heated in our lives. Our faith being strong allows us to operate with the Holy Spirit inside of us and we become extinguishers in the kingdom. We will be able to extinguish "all," not some but "all" of the flaming arrows of the evil one, as it explains to us in the word of God (Ephesians 6:16").

MY TRUE IDENTITY

Identity is the fact of being who or what a person or thing is. It is the distinguishing character or personality of an individual.

You discover your identity and purpose through a relationship with Jesus Christ.

A person's identity is his or her own sense of self; of who they are. The way you perceive yourself, your actions, your thoughts, and your interactions with others are influenced by your identity. Your identity has a lot to do with your character; it is who you are.

When I was in the world, I enjoyed the world. I spent so many years living a lie because I thought that the life that I was living was the truth. I was so caught up in enjoying life and partying, smoking weed, getting drunk, and pleasing others. I never really took the time out to read the bible and get a revelation from it. My mind was stuck on the things that helped me get through the day. I was barely making it through the day, and I really didn't know how I fell asleep at night without being drunk and passing out. I woke up with hang overs, dehydrated, and feeling faint more days than I woke up normal. I can remember times that I went to a club and was still under the influence from the night before. My head was hanging and spinning so bad that I had to go to the emergency room. When I got there, I found out that I had alcohol poisoning. I never thanked God for the fact that he kept me through it all, and I didn't die. I had been saved before, and I knew that I was always saved but the attack was real when it came down to alcohol. I had an addiction and I didn't know it until I rededicated my life to Christ. Being addicted to something is like being enslaved to a habit.

My identity in the world was actually a person that was sick and lost. Addiction is a primary, chronic disease.

I had some serious issues, and I needed help, but the devil had my mind so caught up in thinking that I didn't have a problem. I woke up every day without a plan that could help me grow. As long as I was enjoying myself, I was comfortable with the lifestyle that I was living.

In the first chapter, I talked about my issue which was anger. My identity was a person who was angry most of the time and never really cared about what people had to say concerning me, but truth was, I needed deliverance. I knew that I needed deliverance from alcohol, drugs, anger, and a poverty mindset, but I didn't know that I needed deliverance from the opinions of others. I actually did care, that is why I was so angry about every negative or positive thing that others had to say concerning me. The opinions of others can either make you or break you. People focused more on who I used to be than who God created me to be. When folks don't know God, they don't understand purpose. Being a person of poverty caused me to not be able to think on a more realistic level. I thought I was poor and I would never be able to get some of the opportunities that others were offered. I came up in a low income based home and we only had what we needed. There were times that the Lord blessed my mom and dad with extra and we were able to get what we desired, but we had to earn them first. I couldn't get the shoes, clothes, or gadgets that my friends had because the prices would put a dint in my family's budget. We lived in places that were based on our income, so when I turned 18, that was what I applied for; based on my income housing or affordable housing. I didn't apply for anything other than that because that was all that I was exposed to. That was all that I knew. I didn't graduate from high school or pursue my GED because there were family members around me that didn't seem to care much about it either. We had a mentality that was based on settling and being comfortable with what we had as long as we were comfortable. I had plenty of good job opportunities without degrees, so I felt like I didn't necessarily need it anyway. There were a lot of woman in my family that were single parents and never married. If they were in relationships, they were comfortable with dating for 20 and 30 years because nobody really stressed the fact that fornication was not acceptable in God's eyes. No one explained social security or retirement or even 401k for that matter. We were raised to work and that's it. "Get money"! We knew growing up in church that fornication was wrong, but no one really put emphasis on it and besides, we only knew what we were exposed to. I had grown up seeing other adults doing it, so I did it too. Like I mentioned before, we only know what we are exposed to.

When I went through a mind renewal , I asked the Lord to show me what my true identity in Christ was. I no longer wanted to continue living less than what God had purposed me to be. I didn't want to raise my kids the same way that I was raised. The bible says to "Train a child up in the way that they should go and they will not forget that path." That is what I wanted to do. Exactly what the bible says to do. Whenever you raise something (like a plant) or someone, you just make sure that they/ it, has everything that it needs in order to live, but when you train them, you teach them how to do it on their own. You show them the steps and you teach them something so that they can do it on their own. When you teach a child something, the younger they are, the quicker they will catch on. It also has a lot to do with the interest in a place or thing. Children like to learn new things and they like to see their accomplishments as well as be rewarded for them because they like to be proud of themselves. They like to be celebrated and told whenever they have done a good job instead of just when they have made bad decisions. Once I started training my kids instead of raising them, I exposed them to things other than poverty. My identity changed. I was no longer just a mother. I became a teacher, a mentor, a counselor ,coach and a trainer. I taught my kids to be better than I was and to be young women of God that were seeking the kingdom of God. They learned what purpose is, and they sought God to hear his voice concerning their lives. They started being more concerned with finding out what their identities in Christ were. When I was in the world, I was always a leader, and I knew that the Lord had called me to lead, but I never knew that I was called to lead a spiritual group of people. My identity consists of being a bold, strong, African American woman that not only follows Christ, but allows Christ to live inside of me every day. My identity is a woman who is purposeful. I am a child of God, and I am fearfully and wonderfully made as it is said in Psalms 139 :14. My identity is a woman who is seeking ye first the kingdom of God and trusting him to add to my life according to his will. My identity is a person who is passionate for others who are lost and striving to know who Jesus is. I met people that the Lord showed me that I was assigned to. I had some days that I had to press on, no matter what I was feeling like because there were people that lives really depended on my condition in the kingdom. Many are called, but few were chosen. I am one of God's daughters that was chosen to carry on a great assignment. I have to be willing to rebuke myself and allow the Lord to use me as a vessel 100%. I am not the person that the devil tries to make me out to be. I was not a person that accumulated jail charges or walked around hopeless or angry. Neither was I an unforgiving person, bitter, resentful, and holding on to things of my past.

I asked the Lord to help me figure out my identity in him. It was very clear who I was in the world, but that did not tell me who I am in Christ. My identity in Christ is the person that I needed to be to help me build a tight relationship with Jesus, repent, gain salvation, and have everlasting life. The person who I was in the world had to die completely. No longer could I walk around working for the devil and thinking that I could reap the benefits of Jesus at the same time. I had to choose one or the other. The person who I am in Christ could no longer engage in foolish activity or wickedness. I had to change the places that I went, the people that I fellowshipped with, the conversations that I had, and the way that I perceived things. I had to get my priorities together. That was basically how I begun seeking the kingdom of God. I had to know what was more important than others and figure out what needed to be done first and foremost.

I started to engage in the word of God more than I used to. My pastor used an example of engagement when it relates to a companion. He said that when we are engaged, we want to call our companion every chance that we get. We check on them, we make sure that we understand them, we find out what it is about them that we need to know, we cover them, we love them, and we always want to be in their presence. We are intimate with them, and we basically can't get enough of them. That is how we should be with the word of God. It should become our everything. We should be trying to get more and more of it as we grow in God. The word of God helps us grow spiritually.

Acts 19:20 says: "In this way the word of the Lord spread widely and grew in power."

This bible verse is proof from the bible that the word of God causes us to grow in power, especially if you act upon it and use it. My identity had to be a person that pleases God. I had to grow in power. In order to do that, I had to be more like Jesus. Jesus is the only one that pleased God, so why not be like him, live like he does, and have his identity? My true identity in Christ allowed me to see what was inside of me. In 1 John 4:4, it says, "Greater is he who is in me than who is in the world." Jesus is in me; the Holy spirit. The person who was in the world had to do a lot of fighting to defend herself, but the person who is now in Christ fights also, just not physically off of the hands, only in spirit. I don't have to. I have the Holy spirit who is a comforter, and he does the fighting for me. Jesus promised to send help when he went away, and he made it clear that he would return again. By me receiving the Holy spirit, I was able to be considered one of God's children.

I believe that Jesus died on the cross for my sins and rose on the third day. John 1:12 says: "Yet to all who did receive him, to those who believed in his name, he gave the right to become children of God."

My true identity in Christ is a child of God. Through Jesus Christ, I was adopted into God's family, so I am now his child.

Ephesians 1:5 says: "He predestined us for adoption to sonship through Jesus Christ, in accordance with his pleasure and will."

My true identity in Christ came when I realized that my old self was crucified with Jesus on the cross so that my body that was covered in sin would die. I became free from a slave in sin once I was saved by Christ.

The bible also explains this in Romans 6:6: "For we know that our old self was crucified with him so that the body ruled by sin might be done away with, that we should no longer be slaves to."

Many people struggle with the answer to the question, "Who am I"? Who you are says a lot about what your purpose in life is, and what is important to you. I've learned that I made the mistake in the past by basing my identity on what I do, like my job, or my role in relationships. I let those things define me, but they actually were putting limits on my life. As a Christian, my identity encompasses all the abundance of being a beloved child of God. My role as a

Christian is to be a saint, not a sinner, and I can always count on Jesus' help to overcome sin in my life. I can rely on Jesus' help to help me resist temptation, and if I do sin or fall short, all I have to do is confess and repent. To repent is to turn away from it and never do it again. As a Christian, I had to maintain a humble attitude and have gratitude for God's grace. I know that I am blessed. The greatest blessing that I have is God himself as my father and he loves me. I can walk in confidence knowing that God is with me always and everything that happens in my life will work out for the good as long as I trust him. God brings so many different blessings in my life , and I have to make it a habit of making him a priority every day.

Here are a few ways that I discovered my true identity in Christ. I realized that I did not do things the same way that I used to and my perception of things were totally different than they were in the world. I had the word of God that sustained my spirit and reminded me that my true identity was not who I was before I received Jesus as my Lord and savior. It's certain things that I know now that give me the confidence that I need to know who I really am in Christ.

Knowing my identity is knowing for a fact that I am appreciated by God. He notices every good choice that I make in my life even when no one else does. I don't have to get weary in well doing because in due time, I will reap the harvest . One way of showing God that I appreciated him was, I had to exchange my grumbling for praying, my competing for celebrating, bitterness for thankfulness, performing for serving, and my boasting for encouraging.

My true identity knows that I am saved thanks to Jesus' sacrifice on the cross for me. I know that I am saved from sin, death, Satan, my old human nature, and my old pattern of worldly living. I show thanks to God by showing gratitude and doing good works that God has planned for me to do to fulfill my purpose. I had to help others discover and build relationships with him to help redeem his word.

My identity today says that I am reconciled. Jesus has spiritually reconciled me to God and other believers. God plans for all Christians to live together in heaven no matter what our backgrounds or issues are. So therefore, I have to do my best to live Holy and ask him to help me be peaceful, humble, and compassionate towards other people because that is the way he is for us. I have to remember that God hears me and he responds to my prayers when I am connected to Jesus. I can't get to God except through Jesus because he is God's son, and he gave full instructions for us to listen to him. I feel free talking to Jesus, and expressing myself to him confidently. I always tell him my thoughts and feelings at any time, and I expect for him to listen to me because he cares. I know that he will listen to me and answer my prayers only according to what he knows is best for me.

My true identity knows that I am gifted. God has given me special abilities that he wants me to use in the Christian ministry that he calls me to do everywhere that I go. I realized that my passion was where my purpose was. It wasn't hard for me to understand that I was called to minister to the community because I have a passion for the people. I found out the areas that I was gifted in by asking myself questions like: What do I find joy in doing for others? What opportunities has God already provided for me to serve others? What are the things that I am best in and have the most success in? What has other Godly people, like my leaders commended me for doing? and what acts of service have given me the sense of satisfaction? These questions help me determine the areas that I am gifted in and they help me understand what God blessed me to do or where he has given me grace to have the ability to do things that others may not be able to do.

Knowing my true identity in Christ is knowing that I am new. I am made new in Christ and old things are gone. When I began a new relationship with Jesus, he placed a new spirit inside of me and my old spirit died. So, I am a different person than I was before I became a Christian. However, that does not mean that I won't make mistakes because I am still learning and growing every day, and I will be for the rest of my life, but I will gradually become more like Jesus the closer that I get to him and the more that I engage into the word of a God.

I know for a fact that I am forgiven. I do not live in condemnation because there is no condemnation in Christ Jesus. Jesus paid the price that God's justice demands for my sin and took God's wrath for me upon himself. I am forgiven for all of my sins, past, present, and future. One of the ways that I show Jesus gratitude for forgiving me is by obeying God's commands by forgiving people who have harmed me and seeking forgiveness from God for people that I may have harmed.

I have to keep in mind that I am rewarded by God. God will

reward me for everything faithful and holy that I do as a Christian. Although I can't earn my salvation. After I got saved, I became eligible to earn rewards for my obedience and submission in heaven. I gain plenty of points with Jesus for the work that I do while serving God here on earth.

My true identity in Christ says that I am victorious. Jesus has given me the power to overcome evil, sin, and death. I have to use the spiritual weapons that he has given me to fight; truth, righteousness, the gospel, faith, salvation, scripture, prayer, and the strength from Jesus to be able to stand. I have to trust that I can always emerge victorious.

Knowing your true identity in Christ is having a benefit of self-knowledge. To know yourself is the beginning of wisdom.

When you know yourself you have:

1) HAPPINESS

2) BETTER DECISION MAKING

3) SELF CONTROL

4) RESISTANCE TO SOCIAL PRESSURE (you are less likely to say "yes" when you want to say "no"

5) A BETTER TOLERANCE AND UNDERSTANDING OF OTHERS

This step definitely changed my life. Knowing who I am in Christ helped me figure out what I really needed, and it showed me my struggles as well as my strengths. It revealed the gifts and power that the Lord has given me to get through the things that have beat me down in the past. If I knew who I was years ago, I feel like I would be much farther than I am today, but I don't regret the process, because it takes a process for us to be where God has planned for us to be. You have to earn your keep, and experience is the best teacher. Once you have gone through a process, you appreciate things better than if they were just handed to you on a platter. You will never forget the hard work that you put in to be who you are in Christ, and you will respect the fact that God made you greater and he holds you accountable to be everything that he created you to be

HEARING GOD

I learned so much going through my process, and I am still learning things and going through a different process every day. Each level gets higher and higher, and I go from faith to faith and glory to glory. The act of waking up and getting dressed, starting my day, and getting my priorities in order is a process. It is not easy at all for me to ignore the fact that I am still capable of falling down on my face or making a mistake here and there. I begin my day with prayer and meditation, and I try to pray as much as I can throughout the day. I make sure that after I finish my day, I do what is required of me as a mother for my kids and grandson. Then I shower, get ready for bed, and pray and meditate again. In the year of 2016, I really learned the importance of meditation and meditating on the word of God. Being still is a part of meditation. Most of the time I found myself running around seeing about the needs of others and not seeing about myself. I was running all day off of maybe one meal and a Gatorade to keep myself from suffering from dehydration. I was abusing God's holy dwelling temple which he refers to as my body. If I didn't take care of it, then who would? When I finally set a time each day to sit still and talk to God, I started to change tremendously. The act of breathing in your nose and out of your mouth can help you so much. Especially when you are paying close attention to your respirations.

The definition of meditate is: To think deeply or focus one's mind for a period of time, in silence. To think deeply or carefully about something.

Once I started reading the bible and meditating, I began to get a better revelation of what it was saying to me. Words were no longer just words, and situations were not just situations. I thought deeply about every bible story and every word that was written because I realized that every word meant something important for my life. I discovered that if I expected to get the most out of my studying, I had to slow down and really think about what I was reading first. I couldn't just read or quote scriptures without knowing the depths of what I was reading. I had to have a understanding of what I was reading before I could even begin to get a revelation. Meditation allowed me to hear God as he spoke to me concerning what I was studying. I think about how well meditation works for me now, and I wish I had practiced meditating when I was younger and in school. I could have passed many tests and solved many problems if I had just slowed down and listened for God's answers. I didn't only use meditating for reading the word, but I started to use it for prayer as well. I had to be still and hear God with peace and silence before I could even open my mouth. I prayed in my heavenly language (tongues) allowing my spirit to pray for me because I had no clue what to pray about. Once I reached this step to my process, I found myself doing more listening and meditating instead of talking in my prayers. My prayers went from asking God for things to just listening to him speak to my spirit as he calmed me down after so much chaos or the struggles of the day alone. I would worship God in my prayer time to show him that I appreciated who he was.

I created a comfortable space in my home where I had laid pillows and a blanket on the floor. I made my space comfortable so that I could relax and receive from the Holy spirit. I had to cut off all distractions like phones, alarms, the TV, and outside connections because I didn't need any interruptions what so ever.

1) I knew my identity in Christ.

2) I knew how to humble my spirit.

3) I understood what my issue was so I did what I had to do to get the spiritual counseling and therapy that I needed.

4) My faith was activated. There was nothing at all that anyone could convince me to make me feel like things were not working in my favor.

5) Transformation had taken place, so I was no longer the person that I was in the world.

6) I received salvation. My old person died. Jesus was resurrected

inside of me and I no longer made decisions for myself. The Holy spirit used my body and worked through me.

7) I learned how to accept the things that I could not change and I had great expectations concerning God.

There was one thing that I still had trouble with, and that was hearing God's voice. Meditation opened up a door for me to be sensitive to the atmosphere. I heard God in many other instances, but I never waited to hear the end of the instructions. I was so happy about hearing a different voice that I would jump and move so fast and end up stuck. I ended up stuck because I didn't wait to hear the end. I remember hearing God say, "Go and feed the poor, " but I didn't wait to hear the instructions telling me "where to go." I heard God say "Separate," but I didn't wait to hear him tell me" who ,what ,and where to separate from." I heard God say for me to plan a "Taking Intersession to the Streets Program," but I didn't wait to hear "when." There were times that I would quit jobs or stop associating with people because I thought God had instructed me to do so, but I didn't wait patiently to hear exactly what he meant.....I moved too fast.

Through my meditation, God had shown me myself. I was reaching for a hand that was reaching for me as well, but I just couldn't seem to grip it. I continued to meditate longer each day and I sought the face of God to show me what this vision meant that I was seeing. I read the word daily and I asked the Lord, "What is it that is keeping me from gripping these hands that seem to be reaching down from heaven?" I was aggravated about not moving into places that I felt I was supposed to be in, and I thought that God had forgotten about me. I had to be reminded over and over again that God is in control over everything because he is the creator. The Holy spirit took me to these verses to help me out:

1 Peter 5: 6: "God will exalt you in due time, if you humble yourselves under his mighty hand."

Psalm 89:13-15: "Your arm is endowed with power; your hand is strong ,your right hand exalted .(14) Righteousness and justice are the foundation of your throne ;love and faithfulness go before you .(15) blessed are those who have learned to acclaim you, who walk in the light of your presence, Lord."

Isaiah 48:13: "My own hand laid the foundations of the earth, and my right hand spread out the heavens;when I summon them ,they all stand up together."

Jeremiah 32:17: "Ah, Sovereign Lord, you have made the heavens and the earth by your great power and outstretched arm . Nothing is too hard for you."

I imagined this hand that I saw in my meditation to be God's hand stretching out to help me. These verses had spoken to my spirit as comfort to let me know that God's hand is powerful and it would keep me safe from harm in my time of trouble. Nothing is too hard for God. I think that this is why the Lord was showing me the image of the hand. I really used to walk in fear because I didn't understand why I was seeing myself struggling to grab God's hand. I thought that it was good to grab God's hand. When I was coming up, the church would always sing a song " Hold on to God's unchanging hand." That meant to me that his hand remains the same. It never changes. It doesn't matter when I call him or reach for him; he would pick me up. But this wasn't happening in the vision that I was seeing. So, I went to bed after the meditation and I woke up with my heart feeling heavy. My soul was weary. I felt as if God was upset with me or something. I didn't know what I had done wrong for him to not grab my hand in the vision. The Holy spirit took me to another verse and it was :

Ecclesiastes 7:18: "It is good to grasp the one and not let go of the other. Whoever fears God will avoid extremes."

The Lord was speaking concerning me taking hold of his word and embracing it. Practicing it and not withdrawing my hand from it. I had to learn to keep God's commandments and please God; walking by the rule of his word so that I could be delivered from all extremes and all of the evil consequences of them. God avoided all of the inconveniences in my life. My instructions were to never withdraw my hand from God's instructions. Wisdom will strengthen the wise and true wisdom will teach me to fear God and to keep close to the rule of my duty as a child of God. Keeping a hold to God's hand; which is his word, supported me better when I was faced with trouble, and it secured me more effectually against dangers. God's hand is the support that never fails, verses my own strength that is weak alone. I thought that I had mastered everything that I needed to do in the first seven steps of this book but what I failed to realize was that the process involved much more work. I wasn't quite there yet. I had been through different experiences, obstacles, and challenges, but I had some more things to do so that I could hear God clearly.

The vision that God had given me was not to physically grab his hand, but to spiritually take hold to his word, with his word representing his hand directing me in the direction that I needed to go. God wants me to practice it, as well as know how not to let go of it. People get many different revelations from this, but I thought that it was amazing that God was basically showing me that I had kept putting my hands on the plow and looking back. I had a problem with looking back and having doubts about my destiny. The bible also states this in:

Luke 9:62: "No one who puts a hand to the plow and looks back is fit for the kingdom of God."

During my studying of plowing, I discovered that a person who plows has to keep their eyes straight ahead or they will blotch the job. There was an example given to me about a girl that was learning to drive. She rode past some friends and she waved at them so that they could see that she was driving. Cars (just like lawn mowers) tend to only go in the direction that you are pushing or driving them and you have to be looking ahead of you to steer them without an accident taking place. She ran up on the curb and popped the tire, while knocking over the fire hydrant and all. This example allowed me to see how you can lose focus and get completely off track. Not only will you get off track, but you will mess up some things along the way. I had to pay attention to pay attention, focus on my mission and stop focusing on being seen or worrying about the things that were going on around me. It is good to be celebrated, but the Lord teaches us to be doers and servants. It is also good to celebrate others. Whatever you make happen for others, God will make happen for you.

Once I had thought things through about my journey and I knew the right things to do, I couldn't keep second guessing things. I had to think things over carefully and be very wise about making decisions that I may regret later. I've learned now that once I've determined the right things to do, just do it. Second guessing myself when the path is clear and things are obvious can only leave me with feelings of defeat.

Once I agreed to allow Jesus to operate in me and through me, I had decided that I was going in the same direction that he wished to carry me. I couldn't worry about my mom, dad, sisters, brothers, friends or anyone else. Once I had put my hands to the plow, I couldn't look back because if I did, then that meant that I was not fit for the kingdom. In order to help build the kingdom, I had to be able to keep my spirit fed and allow the word of God to build me. Building the kingdom involved doing God's will, keeping his commandments. The will of God is the word of God. I had to follow instructions from the bible in order to be sure that I was doing God's will. Reading it and doing it is two different things. I was reading the word, but I wasn't able to take it in and allow it to manifest in my life because I had entirely too much going on. I didn't make the word of God my priority because I had so many other things that I put ahead of it that were not .

I basically had too much weighing me down in my vision that I saw during my meditation. One hand was reaching for God and the other hand was loaded down with bags. They were keeping me from being able to reach higher. Too much unnecessary baggage was wearing me down and being a hindrance; causing delays in my life. I was accepting jobs that God never said to apply for and agreeing to assist with different assignments when I didn't even have my own assignments done. I had filled my calendar up with things to do, but I found myself becoming busy doing nothing, going nowhere. Busy, but not effective. It was like I was on a treadmill; running in place. I was moving too fast and I wasn't listening to hear God's next call. I thought I had it all figured out, but I was so unstable. I was off balanced because everything that I had the ability to do seemed like what I should have been doing ,but that was so wrong. I had made it to Step 7 , so I thought that I was ok now. The problem was that I needed to hear God.

I can remember one night that I attended a deliverance service and I was feeling confused in my spirit, so I laid it all at the altar. I had some trust issues because I was at a place in my life where I thought that I was doing everything that I was supposed to do as a Christian. I decided that day I was going to change the way I viewed God. I made up my mind that I was going to sit down somewhere and focus on God and his will only. I stayed out of the way when it came to people, places, or things that caused me to detour away from God's will and I spent as much time that I could building a relationship with God. I had walked into a season in my life that consisted of so many storms at one time. Even though I had been doing what the Lord wanted me to do, I still had to pass some test and overcome some obstacles. I wasn't getting off of the hook that easy. I had to know my father's voice separate from others. God had opened up doors for me that only he was capable of doing. I knew that he was real, but I had put limitations on my beliefs. I couldn't believe what the bible stated in Matthew but not believe what it stated in John. That's impossible and double sided. If I was going to believe the bible, I had to believe all of it. I had an issue with seeing God for who he is instead of what he had already done. After I read more and more about what God had already done and still was doing , my mindset started to change. In my meditation, I stopped asking for stuff and I started showing more gratitude for the things that were living proof. God had already been showing me that he kept his word and he was definitely capable. If he did it before, he could do it again. "He is the same God yesterday, today, and forever" (Hebrews 13:8).

I woke up one morning at six a.m. and I got my daughter up for school. My spirit had been uneasy for about two weeks. I had cried out to God asking him to help me because I had found myself so aggravated and in grief. I still didn't fully understand the vision. The last time that I felt this way, my aunt Stella was in hospice and she was about to transition to be at peace with Jesus. No one was in the hospital or even sick that I knew of at this present time. I had so much that I was trying to do with my life, and I was helping others as a mentor and child of God. The Lord had allowed me to see who was for me and who was against me, so now I knew how to meet folks where they were, and I understood that there was also an order of how I dealt with people. I had to always display Jesus, no matter what. I grew up saying the old saying "Love people from a distance." But if the truth is to be told, if Jesus loved us from a distance, we would be so lost in this world. I had developed a different kind of love once I gained a closer relationship with God. I had developed a love that gave me peace just to think about God. He showed me an Agape love and no one else in this world had ever come close to that.

An Agape love is the highest form of love. It is the love of God for man and of man for God. Agape embraces a universal, unconditional love that transcends, that serves regardless of the circumstances. Agape love is the kind of love that Christ has for us. It was called a sacrificial love. Being loved by God allowed me to love people on a different level. I no longer cared about what people did to me. I would still find myself checking on them or sending my love to let them know that I am still here if they ever need me. I prayed for people that had hurt me in the past and I forgave them so that my heart could be without bitterness. My love for people is amazing now; a love that I had developed while building my relationship with God, and it caused my heart to change in a way that is not explainable. Even though I loved God and I had grown spiritually, I still had some things that I had to work on, and submission was one of them.

I had spoken to God about all of my feelings and in my practice of meditation I found myself hearing his voice more clear. God was there every time that I went through my struggles and he knew exactly what I needed to get better. God was waiting for me to submit my spirit to Jesus. I went through life thinking that I had it all figured out because I refused to submit to anyone at all; not even God. I can remember being in jail when I was younger and in the world, and I blamed God for not letting me make bond or not allowing me to beat some charges that I wasn't in fault for. I was so mad at God, so I told myself that I was not going to do what he wanted me to do because he didn't do what I wanted him to do for me. One day I was tired of guessing about what I thought I was hearing God saying, so I finally meditated on the word of God instead of meditating on my own thoughts, and I found myself reading some scriptures.

John 10:27: "My sheep hear my voice, and I know them, and they follow me."

Jeremiah 33:3: "Call unto me, and I will answer thee, and shew thee great and mighty things, which thou knowest not."

John 8:47: "He that is of God heareth God's words :ye therefore hear (them) not, because ye is not of God."

John 8:47 is the verse that really did it to me. This verse made me understand the reason I could not hear God at that time. The verse was straight up the truth. Self-explanatory. No ways around it. If I couldn't hear him, then I was not of him.

1: I had some ways that I still was harboring, thinking that God couldn't see me. I was still sinning knowing that I was wrong. The verse John 10:27 says that his sheep know his voice. If I claimed to be one of God's sheep, then I shouldn't have had an issue with hearing him.

I asked God questions concerning my life because I was tired of living the same. I asked questions like: What am I going to do with the rest of my life? Where should I go to school to pursue my Ged? Should I take this job, or is there something better on the horizon? Who should I marry, or will I even get married? Life is full of choices and I had to make them whether I wanted to or not. It was much better once I had learned to wait on God and listen for his voice to direct me. Besides, if I claimed to love God, then there should have been no problem being of him and obeying his will. I read an article that was talking about how people really win a star. The question is "Should we look to the stars or should we look to the maker of the stars?" I sought God's face every chance that I was given. I can remember getting off of work and going straight home weeks and months at a time so that I could be in the privacy of my home with just me and God. No interruptions. As I meditated I would breath slowly, breathing in through my nose and out of my mouth. Inhale, exhale. Allowing the breath of God to fill my lungs completely (Genesis 2:7).

Closing my eyes and relaxing every muscle in my body while thinking of everything that had me bound. I rewound the hands of time and I went back a few years to when I wasn't delivered from pain. I thought about the things in life that had hurt me.

1:The people that I had went out of my way for and they acted as if I didn't exist.

2:The relationships that still had a part of me tied to them and made me walk full of bitterness.

3: My past that was chasing me every day, tapping me on my shoulder, begging me to just turn around and come back.

4: My mistakes and all of the paths that I had walked down and gotten attached to things and different spirits that had me feeling like I was stuck.

5: My life experiences with my children and the hurt that they had endured because of abandonment , and rejection from others ;not knowing why things happened the ways that they did and why they were born into a nature of poverty.

Then I opened my mouth and I told God how I felt concerning it all. I finally had a conversation with God about it instead of yelling or blaming him for it.

I first, apologized to God for me not being obedient and not doing what his word had instructed me to do for years. God didn't need an apology because he already knew what my life consisted of and he knew my heart . He loved me as his daughter even with my mistakes. He had chosen me to be purposeful and walk in to some places that only he could take me, so now I just needed to start right where I was and repent for what I had done; turn away and do better. He listened to me without interruptions. He allowed me to lay it all at his feet so that he could pick it all up and do away with it. He already knew how I felt and what I was going through in the past but in order for me to submit I had to let things go 100%. It's hard to submit to someone when you have hard feelings towards them. I thought that I loved God seriously, but I really couldn't say that I loved him if it was so hard to submit. I was too concerned about the things that had gone wrong in my life and I needed to trust God to deal with it.

God wants to fellowship with us and he wants to communicate. Communication is a two way street. Back and forth. The same way we talk and God listens, He talks so we should listen. God loves us so much and he proved it when he sent his only son to die in our place. He did this so that we could have life and we will be able to fellowship with him after this life here is over.

(Hebrews 10:19-20)

God wants us to live a fulfilled life. He wants us to be blessed and successful. In Jeremiah 29:11 He makes it very clear concerning what his plans are for us. In Genesis 3:8 they heard the sound of the lord God walking in the garden. This is how God wants to communicate with us. He wants to walk with us and he wants us to hear him. He wants to really have conversations with us, so he wants us to listen and talk to him too. You can't have a conversation if it's not two or more people talking to each other. God's love letter to mankind makes it clear that we are supposed to have two-way communication with him. When Jesus went away after he rose from the dead, he said that he was going to send a comforter to take care of us and lead us. This comforter is the holy spirit. If we except the Lord Jesus as our savior, we will not have to be lost because now it will live inside of us. So therefore, when we need answers, we will get them.

1 Corinthians 12:1: "Now concerning spiritual gifts, brethren, I would not have you ignorant."

To be ignorant is not having or showing awareness or understanding of the facts; unenlightened, uneducated, unknowledgeable, untaught, or unlearned. The holy spirit does not leave us ignorant. We have knowledge and wisdom once we are born into the family of Christ. Now we can truly consider ourselves God's children. I came to the conclusion that I was going to have to commit and submit . I could finally hear God once I agreed to submit and let him have his way. I wanted to be considered his child. I couldn't see myself screaming "Lord , Lord" and not make it in heaven.

The Lord spoke to me concerning checking my spirit and getting a spiritual "oil change"! He said I need to be sure that my oil is renewed daily and remember that we do not wrestle with flesh and blood but we fight against spirits from dark places, principalities.

By checking my spirit It allowed me to get myself together and hear God's voice the way that I needed to . I looked for God to talk all of the time but when he speaks ,it's not always his voice. God started speaking to me through others. He started speaking to me through visions and dreams. God spoke to me when my daughter was struggling with some things and she was having to deal with evil spirits that she didn't understand at her young age. I asked the Lord to help me and reveal what it was that I needed to do. I didn't actually hear God's voice but I heard him with my eyes. Everything that was happening in my life concerning my kids, job, house, and relationships was God speaking to me, telling me that I was under attack by the enemy and If I just continued to draw closer to him; seeking ye first the kingdom then I would inherit what he had for me. Peace is what I needed and God had it. Not only did he have it but he is peace. There was no way that I could be his child and not inherit what he has or who he is. Greater is he who is in me. God was allowing things to happen because he had to get my undivided attention. The harder the situation determined how loud he was speaking. He wanted me to use the tools that he had given me and follow the instructions of His word as he spoke to me through the pages.

I asked God "why can't I get the job that you promised me?" Instead of the Lord speaking to me about it with his voice, he spoke to me every time I went on an interview and I got the job until they pulled my background check. I was having to resign the same day that I was hired. God was telling me to do what I needed to do concerning my background and continue to walk in his footsteps. He told me to think before I react from this day forth, because now I have experienced what it feels like to get something that I really needed and have it taken away. But I had to remember that the devil is the one that kills , steals and destroys. God doesn't give us things for us to fail. He just speaks to us through our situations and he chastises us when we have stepped out of his will. The reactions from our actions are considered consequences for the choices that we make . God does not go against our wills so if we choose a road then we will have to deal with what may be ahead. God responds to us according to our relationships with him. It's not that he leaves us ,but he just watches sometimes and he lets us get so far until the heat backs us up.

My children know when they have done something wrong by the way that I respond to them. when they have made me proud I reward them. When they upset me, I sometimes have to get quiet on them. That is the same way that God responds to me. It's not that he ignores me to say that he is mad or anything because he does not get mad at us, but he does get disappointed when we do not operate in faith. God is quiet the same way that I am with my kids when they have disappointed me. He allows that time for me to think about why things are not going right? or why my life seems to be falling apart? He speaks to me through blessings as well. Blessings as far as wisdom, knowledge and understanding. I don't look at material things as blessings because the devil gives us material things too and most of the time it is things that we don't need at all. The things that we end up worshipping and using as idols. The things that change us in the worst ways and make us feel above others, causing us to not be able to walk in humility.

God also spoke to me concerning fornication. I had been praying for a husband for years and I felt l would find him once I got saved. That wasn't so true. I was doing everything that I felt that I needed to do for Christ, but my relationship was not close or intimate enough. Before the man that God created for me could find me, I had to be engaged to the word of God. I had to build an intimate relationship and build the trust up enough for God to trust me. I had been making God a man on the side for so long. Something that we refer to as a rebound nowadays. I would date God and commit to men that would not commit to God or myself. One night I asked God again " why is it that I have to be alone?" Why do I have to live my life without a companion?" God spoke with me concerning getting to know who I was in him and knowing who he is for myself. He said that I knew my identity but I didn't trust my position that he had called me for. I still had some doubts about who I was whenever I was faced with trouble. I had to remember who God is in order to remember who I was.

Once I get that in my head clearly ,then he will allow my husband to find me. The man that God has for me did not deserve to have to deal with me not understanding submission. The only way that I could understand it 100% would be to commit to God first. If I can't submit to God ,then submitting to others was definitely going to be a problem. I had finally agreed to submit to God but God wanted me to get a better understanding of what it was and he had to allow me to go through trial and error to be sure that I had truly submitted. I said that I did but I had to prove it.

Submission is accepting and yielding to the authority of a person or superior. Submission is like a proposal. I thought that submission was just going along with someone and agreeing to everything that they said because of their position. But God spoke very clear when he told me to study submission and learn what it is before I asked him about my husband. In order to desire a husband the way that I did, I had to want to desire to be the wife that a husband needed first. I couldn't just lead a "Women Of Virtue Group" , I had to be one. God was still speaking to me through dreams and books, other people's testimonies, and the word from the bible. I thought that something was really wrong with me or God just wanted me to be alone. I know that God is a jealous God and he doesn't want any one before him but I didn't understand why I wasn't married yet . I mean I told him that I was willing to submit. I really meant it from my heart. I studied the word and I meditated more and more, gaining a closer relationship with God, trying to show him that I meant what I said and I was ready to stop playing games. I was willing to go where I didn't want to go, do what I didn't want to do, and be what he called me to be. I was doing all of these things from the first seven steps of this book but I was doing them without submission. It's possible to follow someone's orders without submitting. I was obeying God because of the benefits.

Finally, submitting to God opened up many doors for me because it allowed me to be able to operate in a different type of anointing. Submitting to him let him know that I agreed with his will for my life and whatever he said was what I was to do. Submission means to obey without second guessing. To be obedient and arrange myself under the divine view point rather than to live according to my old ways of life based on my human viewpoint. It is a process of submitting my own will to God's will. Submission relates to someone with a higher power or someone in authority when You refer to a person. You can also submit to a project, job, church, or assignment because you understand the importance of it getting done or you know how much your life or others depend on it.

Once I figured out what submission was, I was able to submit to God with everything in me. I understand that I needed to practice obedience for the authority that is over me no matter what the authority is. By doing this it will bring a temporal blessing to my life and a great reward later. The highest authority is God. In order for me to be able to submit to my husband I had to make sure that we both were submitting to God's will first.   When I get married, I have to understand that my husband will be placed as authority to be the head over my family. So, I will have to submit to him. God delegates authority to others that he has placed in authority over us, so in order to say that I submit to God I must submit to all authority also.

Submission is also an act of obedience. It goes back to what I said concerning my kids. If they were disobedient, I did not want to listen to anything coming out of their mouths because It was an evil spirit that I was dealing with. I thought about how I felt when my kids didn't obey and then I thought about how God may have felt when I didn't obey. I really wanted to be obedient but there was something that I had to do within in order to understand how. Submission had a lot to do with humbling myself before God so that I could hear him. My heart had to be submissive. I would never know how to truly love my husband the way that God intended for me to without a submissive heart. I had to make a choice to submit to God for the process of growing spiritually. It is impossible to grow in God without submitting to his will. When I received salvation, I received wisdom to carry me throughout my journey. But without obedience and submitting to God's authority, I would have been stuck and lost, not knowing how to be a wife or a woman of God either. God only asked that I submit because he is a loving God and he knows what is best for me. The blessings and peace that I gained through submission and humbly surrendering myself to him daily were gifts of grace that nothing in this world could ever compare to. I was able to hear God better, and I had opened a new chapter in my life that involved great conversations with my father who knows what is best for me. I no longer had to worry or struggle, wondering what tomorrow would bring because God was in control. I had submitted to him so I gave up my will to let his will be done. My ears were open for guidance and the walls that I had put up were torn down. The devil had no place to ruin what God's plans were because now I trusted him to work things out, so he had to back up my beliefs.

I am thankful for this step in my life because I learned a lot through the process. The devil thought that he would keep me stagnant and lost, not knowing how to hear God or submit to anything or anyone for that matter. God heard my cry and he knew the desires of my heart, so he helped me. He didn't always speak with his voice where I could hear him, but he allowed me to hear him by feeling him and seeing the outcome to my disobedience. I also saw the lives of others, and I listened to their testimonies of how they overcame the struggles of feeling like they did not have the ability to hear God. God spoke to me in so many ways, and I feel much better knowing that it was the quiet times that he was walking me through the process. The lonely times that he was with me, and the hard times that he was showing me the consequences of my mistakes while giving me the tools to do better next time. It is so true that when you know better, you do better. Now that I know what it takes for me to hear my father, God, I will continue to obey his will and engage in my word so that I can always be connected to his voice.
Engaging in the word of God allowed me to hear Him better and I was able to receive revelation once I submitted to the Holy spirit.

THANK YOU

Thank you so much for allowing me to share my 8 steps forward to being the woman of God that I am today. My advice to you after reading this book is to trust God and trust the process. Everything in life involves steps, and you can't get to the next level until you have mastered the level that you are on now. Humility is the key to learning and knowledge is needed in order to get a understanding or revelation to know who God is. Don't get so caught up on what God can do because he can do all things but fail. Instead, build a relationship and get to know who he is. Each round goes higher and higher in God. I still face obstacles because the enemy knows that I carry weight that is valuable to God's kingdom, but as long as my spirit is built on the word of God ,there will be nothing that can move me or shake me. God is power and we all have it because we all were created by his hands.

Made in the USA
San Bernardino, CA
26 June 2017